The Erosion of Childhood

The Erosion of Childhood

Valerie Polakow Suransky

The University of
Chicago Press

Chicago and London

The University of Chicago Press, Chicago 60637
The University of Chicago Press, Ltd., London

© 1982 by The University of Chicago
All rights reserved. Published 1982
Printed in the United States of America
89 88 87 86 85 84 83 82   5 4 3 2 1

Library of Congress Cataloging in Publication Data

Suransky, Valerie Polakow.
  The erosion of childhood.

  Includes bibliographical references and index.
  1. Children—United States.   I. Title.
HQ792.U5S87   305.2′3   81-16227
ISBN 0-226-78006-6   AACR2

Valerie Polakow Suransky earned her doctorate
in educational psychology in 1977 from the
University of Michigan. She is a research scholar
at the Michigan Society of Fellows and an
assistant professor in the School of Education,
University of Michigan.

To Shael
my source of inspiration for this book

and

To little Sasha
with whom I have rediscovered the magic of early childhood.

Contents

Foreword

There are a number of different ways of writing forewords. While making no claim that my way is the correct one, I am following my instincts, which I feel are the right ones. Although my way of writing such a foreword may appear quite simple, nevertheless the task, for me, is never an easy one.

Almost invariably I fight, as now, to contain myself rigorously within the limits I set for myself. That is to say, I resist the temptation to analyze, even tentatively, the text for which I have undertaken to write the foreword. What is fundamental here, after having read and reread the text searchingly and with great seriousness, is the necessity to tell the prospective readers about the book's significance, about how moved I was when reading it, and how its pages provoked me to a new awareness and reformulation of some of my own ideas about the ideologization of young children. In the final analysis, what is essential is that I, in writing this foreword, invite the person who comes upon this book in the silence of a bookstore to feel impelled to read it.

This book of Valerie Polakow Suransky, as forceful as the title would indicate, made a profound impact on me in its first draft as well as in its present form. I vividly remember how I was seized by this text, becoming more and more gripped by it as I continued reading page after page, on a New York to Geneva flight three years ago. There were very few pages left unread when I suddenly realized that we were flying over Geneva and I had not yet slept.

During the time I spent in Ann Arbor participating in a memorable seminar at the University of Michigan with people for whom I now feel such strong bonds, I shared many satisfying moments of dialogue with Valerie. She spoke to me with the humility of a good intellectual, discussing her research, her findings, her preoccupations, and her excitement while engaged in the act of discovering new modes of knowledge. Alas for us when we no longer experience these moments of excitement! This dialogue bore witness to the book's significance and gave promise to the meaningful experience that I was to have days later on the New York to Geneva flight, an experience which was repeated this year in the rereading of the early text and in the reading of the additional new dimensions of her book, which I did while recuperating from fatiguing work in my ever beloved city of Recife.

This book is compelling and demands to be read.

PAULO FREIRE

São Paulo
August 1981

Acknowledgments

This book is the culmination of many years of curiosity, excitement, uncertainty, and often despair. It is as much the story of my own struggles as a parent, a working woman, a feminist, and a child advocate as it is a searching examination of the prevailing cultural ideology of childhood and its practices in this society.

As I reflect back over the seven years since I conceived this project, when my first child was a toddler and in need of childcare, I realize how much he and the children of this study have taught me—how it is their actions, their expressions, their gestures, their words, in short, the "dailyness" of their lives that have finally coalesced to form this portrait of a modern American childhood.

The experience of writing this book—the fieldwork, the methodological framework, the theoretical and sociopolitical issues—has not always been easy, and there are many friends and colleagues whom I wish to thank: Bill Cave, teacher and friend, who spent many hours reading the various drafts of this book and whose scholarly critique, continuing support, and wise counsel have been invaluable; Pat Hayot, who first began the field observations with me and shortly afterward left for France—our close friendship and exciting midnight discussions during those early months were an impetus to develop this project over the following years; Biff Barritt, colleague, friend and fellow social science "deviant" who founded our Phenomenology Seminar and whose uncompromising honesty and intellectual curiosity have been a constant challenge to me.

To Anna Rubbo, Mark Chesler, Ann Wood, Maria Garcia, Diane Cottrell, and members of the Phenomenology Seminar, I wish to express my thanks for their comments and assistance and for helping to provide a consistent base of support for myself and others seeking to establish a human science research alternative.

There are two other people who have taught me, through their own example, how to "see" and understand children: Ton Beekman, a leading Dutch phenomenologist whose marvelous research with children is paralleled only by his delight in their ways of seeing and experiencing the world; and Frances Pockman Hawkins, whose own passionate involvement with young children in different parts of this country lends a new dignity to the meaning of teacher and whose wisdom and compassion, expressed in her observational writings, have impressed me deeply.

Now, I turn to my family—my parents, Archie and Golda Polakow, who have been a source of strength and support throughout the writing of this book. The countless hours of proofreading, babysitting, and the last-minute crisis management have all been offered with patience and humor which I deeply appreciate. My children have, as usual, kept me honest, and their appropriate impatience to have a "non-busy" mommy has pressured me to meet my deadlines. Shael has lived through many versions of this book and has helped me in innumerable ways, in selecting names for the centers in part 2 and in counting every page and urging me to finish yet another. Sasha made the long climb up and down the stairs many times each day to steal my pens, hide my erasers, and play with my stapler, and through his constant meddling he taught me to keep my "adult" work in perspective. Finally, a special "thank you" for the completion of this family endeavor goes to my husband and comrade Len. He has breathed the air of *The Erosion of Childhood* as deeply as I have, reading, reviewing, critiquing, and discussing many thoughts I have put to paper. His interest in the themes of this book has been a source of ongoing dialogue between us.

There are several other important people I wish to thank. Dale Jerome, a superb typist, whose enthusiasm and interest in my work and insightful comments about the children were much appreciated. I also remember with wry amusement our "predawn camaraderie" on the porch steps as she typed through the night to help me meet various deadlines. Bill Merhab kindly agreed to translate the preface by Paulo Freire, and I thank him for the fine linguistic skills and the painstaking care he brought to the task. I also wish to express my appreciation to the Michigan Society of Fellows for providing me with financial support to write this book while a Junior Fellow and postdoctoral research scholar in the Society.

Finally, I wish to acknowledge the critical influence of Paulo Freire, whose praxis as a revolutionary thinker and educator changed my view of what was possible.

1

1

The Idea of Childhood

Medieval art until about the twelfth century did not
know childhood or did not attempt to portray it. It is
hard to believe that this neglect was due to in-
competence or incapacity; it seems more probable
that there was no place for childhood in the
medieval world.
                    Philippe Ariès
                    CENTURIES OF CHILDHOOD[1]

The Idea of Childhood

The quest for the meaning of a modern childhood forms one of
the central themes of this book as I seek to explore the ambiguous imagery that surrounds our consciousness of the idea
of childhood. Is childhood itself a social invention or is it a
natural state of being? Has childhood always existed or is it a
social space created by the developing bourgeoisie of postfeudal Europe which came of age during the nineteenth century, a period described by Ariès as the "privileged age" for
this particular division of human life?[2]

If the very idea of childhood itself is a myth, what of the vast
and voluminous body of theories that abound in the social
sciences regarding children's psychosexual and cognitive development, their early education, their learning and motivation, their creativity, their moral reasoning—and so the list of
categories continues. What of the age-segregated institutions
that have sprung up in recent decades to specifically cater to
young children, the growth of child-related literature, debates
on quality childcare, attachment, and mother-child separa-

3

tion? As Robert Coles has put it, "In this century of the child, there is little left, it seems, to say about what does or does not happen to the young."[3] We have psychologized childhood; we have outstaged childhood, never questioning whether, in fact, childhood as an *idea* is a relatively modern invention, created by adults grounded in a particular sociohistorical epoch.

Contrasting Historical Images

The question of the very existence of childhood requires deeper examination from historical, psychological, and cultural perspectives. While Philippe Ariès's seminal work on the social history of childhood continues to provoke a fundamental reformulation of our cultural images of the young, his analysis has been challenged in recent years by several psychohistorians who claim, in the words of Lloyd DeMause, that "the history of childhood is a nightmare from which we have only recently begun to awaken. The further back in history one goes, the lower the level of childcare, and the more likely children are to be killed, abandoned, beaten, terrorized and sexually abused."[4] DeMause claims that social historians such as Ariès have contributed to the covering up of widespread brutality and cruelty to children in ages past and that "masses of evidence are hidden, distorted, softened or ignored"[5] in favor of understanding the social conditions of the time.

However, childhood history is not the easiest of fields to reconstruct, for the interpreter is removed from past events—both in time and in age—and is confronted with a paucity of sources which creates a situation where "crowds and crowds of little children are strangely absent from the written record . . . It is in fact an effort of the mind to remember all the time that children were always present in such numbers in the traditional world, nearly half the whole community living in a condition of semi-obliteration."[6] Furthermore, the realities of household structure and organization, the texture of ongoing everyday lives, are only indirectly accessible through recollection, memory, collective folk wisdom, and isolated biographical and diary accounts—all written by adults, whose own structures of consciousness must mediate "the virtually uncharted hinterland of childhood during these distant centuries."[7]

True to his role of psychohistorian, DeMause argues for a psychoanalytic reading of childhood history and attempts to analyze the psychological principles that have characterized adult/child relations. While one might differ with the psychogenic model he constructs in which he depicts the adult in terms of three historical reactions—projective, reversal, and empathic[8]—the evidence he uncovers for his position serves to paint a grim and somber canvas of cruelty to children through the ages. As he traces the different modes of treatment meted out to children in the West, he documents widespread infanticide in antiquity; the outright sale of one's children as war hostages and slaves; the later sanctioning of infant-abandonment to the wet nurse as an institutional norm for the wealthy as well as the poor; the almost universal practice of swaddling to prevent children from moving their limbs or crawling;[9] sexual abuse; genital play; and the use of night terrors which continued unchecked into proceeding centuries.[10]

While DeMause claims that the historical evidence of brutality toward children leads him to a thesis directly opposed to that of Ariès, we need to question whether this very brutality was not part of the generalized social cruelty of the time. A cursory glance at earlier centuries of our human history reveals that both adults and children, nobility and the poor, were subjected to widespread abandonment, punishment, and mutilation for what appear to us today as minor offenses. A look at Shakespeare's more gruesome tragedies and histories, or at the treatment of children in Dickens's England, lends testimony to the different sensibilities evoked in bygone ages—sensibilities that relate to quite different assumptions about the nature of the human condition. If what DeMause has documented forms part of a larger ethos of human interaction, in a nondifferentiated pattern of social cruelty to all people, *including children*, then his argument in fact confirms, rather than contradicts, Ariès's thesis that the idea of childhood as a separate state is a relatively modern notion.[11] For it is only when we develop a separate image of childhood as a distinctive ontological state that we begin to propound a differential morality that recognizes the special vulnerabilities and needs of the infant and child. And it is precisely this theme of the consciousness and recognition of a particular state and nature intrinsic to childhood as a life phase that Ariès raises to the level of our critical awareness. He claims that the child has not always been a child as such. It is we who have created the child, through specific social and historical conventions which, in turn, are dependent on the variations of class and culture. As late as the seventeenth century,

> people could not allow themselves to become too attached to something that was regarded as a probable loss . . . This feeling of indifférence towards a too fragile childhood is not really very far removed from the callousness of the Roman or Chinese societies which practiced the exposure of new-born children. We can now understand the gulf which separates our concept of childhood from that which existed before the demographic revolution of the previous stages. There is nothing about this callousness which should surprise us: it was only natural in the community conditions of the time. On the other hand, there are grounds for surprise in the *earliness of the idea of childhood, seeing that conditions were still so unfavourable to it* [my emphasis].[12]

Thus, in medieval society, claims Ariès, the *idea* of childhood, carrying with it a corresponding image of the *nature* of childhood, did not exist. As soon as children were weaned (usually between the ages of three and five), and deemed able to live without a nurse or mother, they became participating members of adult society. Clearly a recognition of a first stage of life, which we now call infancy, *was* apparent in these medieval times, but thereafter the dividing line between childhood and adulthood faded. Ariès, in examining the art and iconography of the medieval period, finds, too, that there was no attempt to portray childhood as a separate state; rather, children were depicted as miniature adults. This did not appear simply in the world of pictures but in the actual dress of the period. As soon as the swaddling bands of infancy were abandoned, children were dressed like adults.[13] It was not until the seventeenth century that the children of nobility and of the middle class were dressed in age-segregated outfits, once again depicted in the numerous child portraits of the seventeenth century. This particular change, however, interestingly affected boys rather than girls; for it was the idea of childhood that met the aspirations of parents of the sons of the middle class and aristocracy. The concept of childhood, as distinct from youth and infancy, became the preserve of the bourgeoisie. "Consequently the sons of the middle classes were the *first children* [my emphasis] as they had to be separated off from working activities and sent to school to undergo a long training in preparation for their adult working lives."[14]

It was in this way that the idea of childhood became a class phenomenon. The children of the working classes, the offspring of the peasants and the poor, continued to dress like adults, for no distinctions in their way of life were operative either in dress, in work, or in play.

Consonant with the evolving class-based concept of childhood was the change in the structure of play. Prior to the seventeenth century, play and games were incorporated into the culture of all classes without age segregation. In the late seventeenth century, however, a distinction was made between the games of adults and nobility and the games of children and the poor. Hence, the lower classes were infantilized and the concept of childhood became linked to subservience and dependency. An example of how this image became embedded in the language itself is seen in an eighteenth-century dictionary definition of "child" which included the following: "A woman will say to her servant: 'Child go and get me this or that.' A master will say to his men when setting them to work: 'Come along, children, get to work.'"[15]

We see, then, how the medieval period of "miniature adultism" gave way, during the seventeenth and eighteenth centuries, to a *class-* and *sex-based* idea of childhood which is depicted in the changing patterns of cultural play, of dress, and of work. "The old community of games was destroyed at one and the same time between children and adults, between lower class and middle class. This coincidence enables us to glimpse already a connection between the idea of childhood and the idea of class."[16]

Tracing the evolution of this idea of childhood, we note how the adult depiction of childhood has moved from an ignorance

or formal denial in the tenth century, when artists were unable
to depict a child except as a man on a smaller scale, to a class-
and sex-based image in the eighteenth century, to a centering
of the family around the child in the nineteenth century. And
today in the twentieth century, when the "science of childhood" has come of age, we have moved so far from the distant
past of medieval miniature adultism, have become so ob-
sessed with the unqualified separateness of this period of life,
that we have imposed on the social space of childhood an
emasculating psychologism which has succeeded in alienating the life project of the child from the child's existential
reality. We now separate children from the world of work; we
dichotomize play from work; we deny the significance of the
child's contribution to the cultural forms of everyday life. We
infantilize children's perceptions and "school" their minds
through the domestication of their critical curiosity and
consciousness.

In short, in the modern era of childhood, when every stage
from infancy to adolescence is measured and demarcated with
fine technological precision, we have "progressed" from the
forgetfulness of childhood to the *containment* of childhood.
Children as young as a year old now enter childhood institutions to be formally schooled in the ways of the social
system and emerge eighteen years later to enter the world of
adulthood having been deprived of their own history-making
power, their ability to act upon the world in significant and
meaningful ways. Unfortunately, we too often forget that
"adults will never be able to change life if they prevent children from inventing theirs in permanent contact with the reality of the social world."[17]

The images of childhood that hold sway today are rooted in
particular forms of ideology which relate to contrasting views
about gender, class, and family structure. In the following
sections of this chapter I shall examine several feminist perspectives on childhood, the cultural patterning of work and
play, as well as the image of the child in the social sciences in
order to explore further the current conception of childhood in
the West.

Contemporary Feminist Images of Childhood

The litany of social scientism and the proliferation of early childhood education theory that has burgeoned into a profitable industry in this country is dialectically countervailed by another cult of equally "expert" commentators on the meaning of childhood—the radical feminists who, in turn, advocate the demise of childhood.

Shulamit Firestone's oft-quoted "down with childhood" manifesto in *The Dialectic of Sex*[18] and her blueprint for "the ultimate revolution" do away with childhood as a life phase. Firestone bases her arguments for the "myth of childhood" on the medieval period of miniature adultism depicted by Ariès, and claims that as the medieval age was not conscious of children as distinct from adults, children differed from adults only in their economic dependency. For Firestone too, then, childhood is a social invention which is rooted in the economic aspirations of the postfeudal bourgeoisie and has, under modern-day capitalism, become a functional category for oppression, integrally linked to the development of the nuclear family and the subjugation of women. Hence, "The child within these conjugal limits now becomes important; for he was the product of that unit, the reason for its maintenance. It became desirable to keep one's children at home for as long as possible, to bind them psychologically, financially, and emotionally to the family unit until such time as they were ready to create a new family unit. For this purpose the age of childhood was created."[19]

The age of childhood, in turn, reinforced the "tyranny of woman's reproductive biology," which accounted for her original and continued oppression. Firestone cites Engels's observation that the original division of labor between the sexes was for the purpose of childbreeding and led to a social hierarchy within the family where the husband was owner; the wife, the means of production; and the children, the labor. Yet, she claims that these biological contingencies can be overcome and that the "natural" is not necessarily a "human value." "Humanity has begun to outgrow nature: we can no longer justify the maintenance of a discriminatory sex class system on grounds of its origins in nature. Indeed, for pragmatic reasons alone, it is beginning to look as if we must get rid of it."[20]

Hence, the strategy for the liberation and full humanization of women (and presumably others of humankind) resides in "cybernetic socialism," where the state of pregnancy is eliminated, mother-child attachment becomes taboo, parenthood is superseded by a community of adults whom the child will *choose* to relate to, genetic children are eventually phased out of existence, and the new household contains a regulated proportion (one-third) of children. After a few generations of household living, the special bonds between adults and children are severed. Children are then artificially produced or adopted and the problem of the early physical dependency of children is resolved by evenly distributing them among household members. But note the caveat that Firestone offers: "We must be aware that as long as we use natural childbirth methods, the household can never be a totally liberating social force!"[21] It is artificial reproduction and cybernetic socialism that offer true release from contemporary parenthood, an "anguished hell...crippling the psyche," and creates for the child a liberation from a "childhood (that) is hell!"

Perhaps the most startling aspect of Firestone's analysis and program is the paradox between her own scholarship, committed to the liberation of women, and her uncritical acceptance and naive belief in the power of an advanced technology to work in the service of liberation. To deny one's historical vocation as a human being and relinquish this to the machine is to work not for a revolutionary humanism but rather for an era of dehumanization geared to the creation of technical man or woman, freed, certainly, from the tyranny of biology but also from human attachment, spontaneity, and love, in favor of a nightmarish rationalism and unremitting social alienation from the very bonds that cement human relationships. Children emerge as commodities, as artifacts of production, created by technological experts in the white-coated laboratory of life and the human child that once was, is no more, conceived and birthed with efficiency and precision, surrendered to the metallic cradle of technology, there to form the first tentative attachments with the plastic world beyond.

But what if attachment and love, formed during these early

hours and weeks after natural birth, are the very basis of human culture? Certainly Harlow's famous experiments with primates show us that even monkeys need mothers, that they do form primary attachments, and that they crave warmth and love. What if the blood tie is, too, a universal root of human culture in which social relationships are grounded? Shakespeare's *Titus Andronicus*, set in pre-Christian Rome, dwells with compelling power upon the significance of the blood tie; for Titus, in destroying his own blood, wreaks through that action the destruction of his clan and the downfall of the state. The early Greek tragedies, in various ways, also gave form to this primitive impulse and the primordial meaning of blood which across cultures, through the extended family, the clan, the kinship system, has formed the historical basis for human survival.

Only a Western academic, reared in the intellectual tradition of Cartesian rationalism, could so ethnocentrically propose the tyranny of cybernetics over human and social relationships, which encompass far more than the intellectual masterminding of the end of childhood and the bonds of parenthood.

Firestone's advocacy of the demise of childhood is the most extreme of the radical feminist visions. Variations on this theme appear in the work of Kate Millet, who also constructs an alternative to the patriarchical, proprietary family, the source and cause of women's degradation. Millet, however, proposes that childhood be "taken over" by efficient professionals through the collective professionalization of childrearing.[22] Germaine Greer's solution is rather more exotic— the founding of a baby farm in Italy where the children of the adult community would be housed and visited from time to time by mothers and fathers, taking time off from their busy schedules in North America to jet into Calabria.[23] The "oppressive" role of childrearing and housekeeping would be delegated to a "local family," in which, no doubt, the sexual division of labor would be reproduced, not among the Greer elite but in the peasant family employed to run the farm!

These alternative visions of alternative futures propounded by the feminists of the early seventies are rather bleak— cybernetic conception and infancy or the professionalization

of childhood. Both involve the surrender of the being of the
human child to the mechanistic imperatives of a technology
programmed for so-called liberation and humanization. But,
where is the child in this adult vision?

The place of the child and the social space for childhood
have been analyzed in a more balanced perspective by several
feminist writers of late, who have attempted to reconcile the
often conflictual roles of woman-as-mother and woman-as-
professional. Unlike Firestone they do not advocate the demise of childhood or a disengagement from parenthood as
outlined by Greer and Millet, but rather attempt to analyze the
meaning of parenting and the experience of motherhood. The
family unit becomes the central locus of analysis; male/female
roles in relation to household structure and the social organization of parenting once again underlie certain images of
childhood which are in need of critical examination.

Alice Rossi, in a controversial article, captures the spirit of
the times when she points out that "a very diverse set of
groups now share the common view that the nuclear family
and monogamous marriage are oppressive, sexist, 'bourgeois,'
and sick. Exponents of sexual liberation, self-actualization,
socialism, humanism, gay liberation, existentialism, and certain segments of feminism have joined hands in a general de-
nunciation of the stereotyped 'traditional nuclear family'
although rarely defining what they mean."[24] Rossi also claims
that the literature on alternative family forms focuses almost
exclusively on the adult relationship and variant forms of marriage. Rarely is attention directed to parent-child relations, to
childrearing, or to the perspective and experiences of the
children.

The apparent paradoxical dimension that has characterized
the radical change in sexual roles, childrearing, and family
structure over the past decade is that the call for human liberation and freedom from "biological tyranny" has led to a
peculiar vision of American egalitarianism which is enmeshed
culturally within an ethic of extreme individualism and a
laissez-faire morality. There is no radical critique of the
capitalist mode of production and its attendant social relations,
but rather we see individualism and personal profit run
amok—all in the name of self-actualization. In this alienated

landscape, the pursuit for liberation becomes a pursuit for narcissistic self-fulfillment based on the formerly oppressive male model of competition and dominance to which women have now gained access. Whereas woman was once ally with her child, united by common bonds of oppression, she now assumes the pattern of the dominator class. "Just as the sexual script, so the parenting script [is] modelled on what has been a male pattern of relating to children, in which men turn their fathering on and off to suit themselves or their appointments for business or sexual pleasure . . . Parenting is viewed from a distance, as an appendage to, or consequence of, mating, rather than the focus of family systems and individual lives. It is not at all clear what the gains will be for either women or children in this version of liberation."[25]

In a somewhat different vein, Nancy Chodorow's recent book *The Reproduction of Mothering* takes issue with the prevailing sex-gender system, and examines the psychological and interpersonal needs and characteristics emerging from male/female development and how they specifically create *woman as mother*.[26] In her comprehensive analysis of women's mothering and its reproduction across generations, Chodorow discusses its implications for the sexual division of labor, for sexual inequality, for relations between the sexes, and for the family structure. Her account, embedded in a psychoanalytic paradigm of object relations, is impressive in its originality and sociological reformulation of psychoanalytic theory as it pertains to female development. Her analysis, however, suffers from an all too common nondialectical formulation of mothering. It is children, after all, who create mothers, and the voices of children are sadly absent from Chodorow's text. Children as living, intentional beings are eclipsed as she meticulously attacks the major theories of sex-role acquisition, finally settling for a rationalization and reformulation of a psychoanalytic model of development.

However, as Chodorow herself points out, it is necessary to critically analyze the ideological biases in Freud's theory which now exists as our cultural psychology. Many unsupported assumptions that Freud made about early female development merely reflect his own patriarchal ideology and his seeming condescension and misogyny toward women.[27]

Nevertheless, despite her recognition of Freud's pitfalls, Chodorow still argues that "psychoanalytic theory remains the most coherent, convincing theory of personality development available for an understanding of fundamental aspects of the psychology of women in our society, in spite of its biases."[28]

Since this epistemological framework underlies Chodorow's attempt to explore the nature and reproduction of mothering, we need to question, in a spirit of continuing critical inquiry, the very adherence to a theory of personality development formulated not only in alienation from women but also in alienation from the life-world of children. Psychoanalysis, as with all theory, is merely a metaconstruction of reality constituted in a particular historical moment. In order to move beyond the "truth" of a verified body of culturally "universal" data removed from the ground and source of childhood experience (as indeed was the case with Freud—he did not deal *directly* with children in his clinical practice), we should heed the example of his daughter, Anna Freud, who has consistently advocated the need for direct observation of children.

Chodorow, in failing to locate mothering in the interactional moments between mother and child, develops a provocative but ultimately contextless and abstract argument from outside of the social space of childhood. The problem with this entire epistemological topography, which imposes an adult construction of reality upon the early development and experiences of the child, is that the clinical evidence and the transference process are not critically examined in relation to the social context of the encounter; neither are the class and cultural characteristics of the population in treatment, nor the extent to which predefined psychoanalytic categories extend to the cultural shaping of our language and social practice. It is at this point that Chodorow's psychoanalytic argument for the location of mothering within the sex gender system of an unequal division of labor and production becomes flawed; for when we move it from the womb of a psychoanalytic *Weltanschauung*, we begin to question why she goes to such lengths to disprove the biological and role-training arguments[29] in relation to mothering, and instead rationalizes the issue in terms of a psychoanalytic reading of the sociology of gender and the social organization of parenting. One might ask whether any "theory" can adequately explain such complex and nonoperationally defined experiences as love, attachment, bonding, clinging, and warmth? Perhaps we need to view these theories as metaphor—as metaphor which becomes defunct when it no longer captures the images of lived-experience—and motherhood, fatherhood, and parenthood *are* complex and elusive experiences. The relationship between child and parent (whether biological, adoptive, or surrogate) must take the full ranges of human emotion, human vulnerability, and human love into account. Perhaps these ephemeral qualities and dramatic life-movements are better captured by the words of the poets than by the words of the social scientists, whose present images of childhood are so intertwined with adult visions of development and self-actualization needs that the landscape of childhood is left barren by excessive psychologizing. The only contact we have with childhood is through the mediation of theory *about* childhood. While Chodorow is correct that the current social organization of parenting produces sexual inequality and that strategies for change must include a fundamental reorganization of parenting, we should not forget that the child, too, is part of that life project for liberation.

In the evolution of the various feminist viewpoints, we note a move from the extreme advocacy of the demise and coercive transformation of childhood under "cybernetic socialism" to a critical analysis of prevailing family forms and gender inequalities. Clearly the traditional nuclear family with its attendant social roles must be restructured or transcended if the social organization of parenting is going to reflect new egalitarian roles for men and women. However, the restructuring process is an enormously complex task and is tied in part to the transformation of power and social relations under the existing political economic system. The struggle for the democratization of the family and the elimination of sex hierarchy and privilege can only be successfully waged in a grounded commitment to the children as well as to the adults involved. Self-actualization, without corresponding familial and social commitment by both women and men, merely continues the "script" of domination previously mapped by men as the

dominant cartography of an individualistic ethos of interpersonal relations. Rather than deny and rationalize out of
existence those primary bonds of human attachment formed
in, and replenished by, the fundamentally creative act of
childbirth and childrearing, we should commit them to the
centrality of the life project, and from that basis attempt a
restructuring of inegalitarian sex roles and household organization. This, in turn, demands changes in the workplace—for
both men and women. It is parenthood and childhood that
encompass the first dialectic of praxis upon the world. It is in
that praxis that the seeds of social transformation will be sown.

Unfortunately, neither the historical nor the feminist
analyses of childhood outlined thus far have attempted to
probe the child's own perception and consciousness of the
world. How in the past, and how in the present does the child
see herself—as a child? a miniature adult?* To what extent
have adult constructions of reality misrepresented the historical child, and to what extent do they continue to misrepresent
the child's experience of *Dasein*[30]—of being in the world?

Peter Fuller, in an excellent photo-essay entitled "Uncovering Childhood," addresses precisely this point when he
criticizes Firestone for accepting the child-men and child-
women of medieval iconography as realistic representations of
what these children actually *were* in social reality. "Her account, like the images to which she refers, necessarily involves a *misrepresentation* of the child's physical, bodily
being. Her error goes beyond the immediately physical. If we
are any kind of materialist, we assume that being precedes
consciousness, or that how the child *is* or *was* in the world
determines his or her perception of social reality, his or her
experience. A potentiality for bodily development can thus be
equated with a potentiality for psychological development."[31]

In his analysis of mainstream portraiture of that period,
Fuller discusses how this was a formal depiction projected
onto the child from the outside, a representation embodying

---

* In order to avoid the conventional and rather sexist generic *he* or
the clumsy repetition of *he/she* throughout the text, I have decided to
use *he* and *she* in alternating chapters; hence chapters 1, 3, 5, 7, and 9
use *she*, and chapters 2, 4, 6, 8, and 10 use *he*.

the aspirations for the future—*for what the child could become*—failing to see the child in his present, immediate context. Hence, if we only analyze these portraits and icono-graphic representations of childhood through a formal lens, we can assume that childhood did not exist as such, *or* we can go further and question whether childhood as a condition did in fact exist but was not formally depicted because the genre of representation was portrayed through the future-oriented lens of the medieval adult. Fuller notes that in artists' portraits of their *own* children, the images do denote an awareness of a relatively separate existence, and that these "often seem a long way from the 'miniature adult' conventions. These chil-dren too, exist within the space of childhood."[32]

Thus, when we look beyond the formal and artifactual level of medieval culture, we are made aware of the paradoxes, even in that age, that surround the meaning and representation of childhood. In addition, to take Ariès's social-historical re-search at face value and to ignore, as Firestone and DeMause have done, the careful description he gives of the detailed periods of childhood (e.g. infancy, which during medieval times was a period lasting seven years and comprised what we now call early childhood) and to ignore his discussion of the paideia of the ancients and of Hellenistic civilization is to distort the ambiguities surrounding the medieval family in favor of a position that either denies the "historicity of child-hood"[33] or extracts it from the community conditions of the time.

The preceding discussion of both the historical and feminist images of childhood indicates the degree to which the quest for the meaning of childhood must be retrieved from adult structures of consciousness that are fixedly punctuated by a linear, "rational" epistemology of human development. If childhood was acknowledged in the world of the ancients, formally denied in the medieval period, only to reemerge in postfeudal Europe, does a dialectical approach not require us to understand these "centuries of childhood" as a changing historical movement in consciousness directed toward the human future? Furthermore, if we really wish to explore the meaning and existence of a modern childhood, do we not need to obey the famous phenomenological injunction of Husserl and "go to the things themselves," in this case the children, and attempt to understand their structures of consciousness and ways of perceiving their existence?

While this injunction will be pursued in later sections of the book, I now wish to explore a specific dimension that highlights the gulf between a modern and a historical childhood—the world of work. After examining the place of children in the work life of their parents and also as cruelly exploited factory laborers during the industrial revolution and beyond, I contrast the reality of child-as-worker with present-day images of children in the social sciences.

The World of Work

In the manufacture of glass, too, there are jobs which do not appear to harm male workers very much, but are injurious to the health of children. The work is heavy, the hours of labor are long. There is much night-work and the workshops are very hot (100 degrees to 130 degrees F). These factors—particularly the last—weaken the physique of children and lead to stunted growth. They suffer especially from eye-trouble, bowel complaints, bronchitis and rheumatism. Many of the children are pale. Their eyes are inflamed and they often go blind for weeks at a time. They suffer also from violent nausea, vomiting, coughs, colds and rheumatism. When removing glassware from the furnaces the children often work in such heat that the boards on which they are standing, burst into flames.[34]

Friedrich Engels, writing on childhood in the English potteries, paints a horrifying canvas of the bitter oppression of children under industrial capitalism. Here, the childhood of the bourgeoisie and the rich was acknowledged through extensive education and schooling, but childhood for the poor involved an accepted pattern of child labor under brutal conditions. It was not until pressure from philanthropists and religious workers in the nineteenth century began that the idea of childhood was entrenched in the law and institutions of the state in order to advance much-needed reforms for the protection of children's safety, health, and well-being.

There was another side to work, however, and that involved the integration of the child within the household, which functioned as an economic unit. Modern children are separated from the world of work, but before the industrial revolution children were indispensable to the family unit, for most work was done around the home in the form of apprenticeship, and the household itself formed a productive unit. With the advent of the industrial revolution, the factory replaced the family in its productive relations and the world of work was dichotomized from the life of the family, causing great social disruption. Interestingly, the early working class in England actually defended child labor precisely because certain aspects preserved the traditional bonds between children and parents, particularly between fathers and sons.

Opposition to the exploitation of the child worker and the dehumanizing effects of child labor led social reformers to take working-class children out of the factories and put them in schools.[35] This change in the role of the child as a productive member of the household unit, and the placement in an age-segregated institution, changed the social form of the family and in time was to have far-reaching implications for the idea of childhood.

Following the industrial revolution, at the turn of the century, mass education developed, evolving rapidly to meet the needs of industrial employers for a disciplined, skilled labor force. Schooling in capitalist society thus began to serve as a training ground for the industrial workplace, as a maintenance institution providing a mechanism for social and political control. Schools have now become holding places, structuring the child's consciousness in preparation for the adult world of work but simultaneously denying the child the right to participate in meaningful labor, thereby further emphasizing the strict demarcation between the role and production function of adults and children.

We note, in modern-day schools, how children are trained to do "work," but the work is atomized, disconnected from the existential universe of which children are a part; the "work" of learning knowledge is reduced to mere bureaucratic transference. In this way the school becomes a knowledge market, and the teacher a specialist selling and distributing packaged knowledge to the student consumer.[36] The process of education thus becomes an act of depositing, of banking isolated pieces of information into the tabula rasa mind of the students, whose task is not to integrate this knowledge into an ongoing life project but rather to regurgitate these frozen pieces of information when the desired response is required at a future point in time. Paradoxically, in a capitalist society, education is separated from work while ostensibly training the child for work.

Marx, in developing his theory of alienation, argued that work is the mode basic to the development of the self and that while man is *of* the world, he changes and transforms his world through his labor. Through work, man makes his own history, creates and gives form to an authentic praxis upon the world. Hence, "work" under the new communism was envisioned as meaningful, fulfilling, and fully humanizing of man's vocation, in contrast to the social alienation and exploitation under capitalism. In fact, in the *Communist Manifesto* Marx and Engels advocate the abolition of child labor in its present form, to be replaced by free education for all children combined with industrial production. Hence, Marx did not envisage the separation of the child from the work force but rather the integration of the child into a community of workers for whom work and education were meaningful and significant forms of the life project. These ideas have reportedly been translated into successful educational praxis in post-revolutionary societies such as Cuba, Guinea-Bissau, and Mozambique and in the Israeli kibbutzim.[37]

What are the social consequences for modern children whose schooling under capitalism prepares them for the replication of the political order and the reproduction of the social division of labor—where schooling is geared to "maintain the submersion of consciousness; (as opposed to an education that) strives for the emergence of consciousness and critical intervention in reality"?[38]

The school separates the child not only from the adult but from fellow human children of different chronological ages, all of whom, isolated in institutions of learning, are deprived of meaningful action upon reality and denied their history-making power to act upon, and transform, the landscape of the microworld. Their structures of play are artificially fragmented so that play—that ontological mode essential to the development of human culture and, even more, to the development of the evolving human child—is regulated by the demands of the institutional curriculum to produce work. Play and work undergo a false dichotomization, and central forms of the play life of the child are structured out of her experience under the illusion of the false consciousness surrounding work. This lack of awareness of the work-play dialectic in the lives of children, particularly of the very young, is a fundamental theme of a modern childhood, with far-reaching implications for culture and social praxis. I return to this dialectic in chapter 9, there to elaborate more fully the configurations of this theme, grounded in specific childhood contexts.

The Image of Childhood in the Social Sciences

But even if a group of intensely speculative psycho-
analysts have let themselves get carried away; have
resorted to nothing less than a series of wild or
exuberant flights of fancy; have imposed their
theoretical will, so to speak, upon babies, not yet
able to speak or understand words, hence tell what
is on their minds or comprehend what is on the
minds of those around them—still, it will surely be
of some significance for those future social historians
who will be trying to figure out this age, that such a
line of conjecture could not resist the youngest of
the young, and could be offered to the world in
the name of science itself.[39]

It is an interesting historical paradox that childhood, with the vast array of social forms attributed to it across the centuries, has now become the most analyzed and overstaged life phase in our developmental cycle. The plethora of social psychological epistemologies (the psychoanalytic, the cognitive, the behavioral, etc.) all attest in varying degrees to the impositional structures of consciousness that an adult world of "experts" has unquestioningly brought to bear upon this life phase of childhood which Donald Vandenberg has simply and eloquently described as "a becoming at home in the world."[40] How to "become at home in the world" is a formidable task for

the modern child of the West, born as she is to a world ridden
with competing social scientists, vying for theoretical ascen-
dancy and prescriptive power over a generation of parents and
teachers who have surrendered their powers of "knowing"
and "seeing" to the professionals, whose cult of expertise extends from the cookbook recipes of the do's and don'ts of toilet
training to the entrenchment of programs in schooling institutions from the nursery through high school.

As Robert Coles has ironically commented: no child is
allowed simply to play anymore, to develop an occasional
grudge, or even to just happen to get into a fight. These events,
which are rather ordinary in other cultures and were so at
other moments in our own, are now seen, seized upon, and
interpreted through the lens of an alienating psychologism.
We appropriate these everyday life experiences from the
child, distort them from the social context in which they orig-
inate, and, by this appropriation, construct an extensive body
of theoretical data and generalization, alienated from the
original life-world of the child actors themselves.

This century has seen the birth, death, and resurrection of
both Freud and Piaget, only to be supplanted by behaviorism
and various "neo-breeds"; we now hear of the neo-Freudians,
the Freudian-behaviorists, the cognitive developmentalists,
the neo-Piagetians, the stage theorists, and other such "scientists," all of whom share in common *a view from above* which
structures our image of childhood and permeates our educational institutions with often crippling effects.

As it is not possible within the confines of this chapter to
offer a critique of all the contemporary imagemakers of the
science of childhood, I will mention only some salient criti-
cisms and trends.

Psychoanalysis, as with other worldviews, embodies a
particular view of social reality which, in turn, colors our images of childhood. In *Civilization and Its Discontents*,
Freud's reformulation of aggression and his conferring of
equal status upon aggression and libido had far-reaching results. The major emphasis of psychoanalysis shifted to aggression and the analysis of negative transference; hence, "civilization depended on the taming of aggression, rather than on
the sublimation of sexuality."[41] This, in turn, led many

analysts to a preoccupation with children's manifestations of the aggressive drive; but the more sensible, like Anna Freud, advocate sensitive, direct observation of children as a necessary prerequisite for understanding the inner world of the child. Anna Freud points out that the analysts' conception of the aggressive drive is still clouded by the concept of the sex drives, and that there is a tendency *to place clinical results* within the framework of instinct theory rather than *to permit theory to emerge from clinical observations* (my emphasis).[42]

These views have clouded our perception of young children. Inter-child aggression is considered part of everyday life in many cultures, including lower-class subcultures in this country as evidenced by Roger Abraham's analysis of aggression and the disequilibrium norm of lower-class black street culture.[43] This same finding is evident in the participatory phenomenological study of a lower-class Mexican-American community conducted by Emilia Rojo with three generations of families.[44] (See also my analysis of this phenomenon in chapter 9.)

These simple (some might say), natural, aggressive acts in the family and school are seized upon by middle-class analysts and analyzed out of all proportion to context. The socialization function of the school thus becomes the training of so-called disruptive impulses and their channeling into socially useful activities. Dependent upon who is the defined and who defines, generations of children are medicated out of consciousness, or manipulated like Pavlov's dogs and Skinner's pigeons, to submit to a regimen of reinforcement and extinction contingencies in order to bring about the desired behavioral effects.

The *social learning theorists*, jumping on the socialization bandwagon, view socialization as a process designed to achieve the conformity of children to certain social norms and rules. Hence, effective strategies developed through observational learning of captive children in laboratories set out to modify aggressive behavior. The social order is a given, a base from which to work at modifying undesirable behavior in the services of the social system. Society's sanity is accepted as a given, and it is the individual who must adjust and accommodate. Hence, a "blaming the victim" pattern develops whereby "problematical" or "deviant" behavior is analyzed in such a way that the cause is found to lie in the deficient characteristics of the victim rather than in structural or systemic defects.

Observational learning is not critically examined, nor is the underlying basis of the values that the models are imparting, but rather the question becomes how best can we get the child to identify effectively with the model. Elaborate consideration is given by two such pioneers in the field, Bandura and Walters,[45] to imagery formation, periods of exposure, representational systems (imaginal and verbal), attentional and retentive processes; yet no self-reflective critique of the assumptions underlying this manipulated process of child conditioning is evident.

The growth of *behaviorism*, which viewed the child as a biophysical being, an extension of the animal, without intentionality or active consciousness, has been the most pragmatic and functional of psychological ideologies to date, and followed an illustrious decade of American experimental psychology where the likes of Thorndike, Hull, Watson and Skinner strutted across the stage of the new science of behavior.

Learning became a central focus of behaviorism, in which data testing took place through animal conditioning. The study of *behavior*, to which learning and most human action was reduced from the complex to the simplest examinable element, became the key methodological tenet. A set of functional relations was assumed to exist between the environment and the behavior of the organism (be it rat or child—no matter!) and soon a "science" of behavior was founded on the observable, measurable manifestations of human life. Hence, language, for Watson, was described as "mere motor sounds in the larynx" followed by atomistic operationalism which defined learning behavior, feeling behavior, imagination behavior, linguistic behavior in stimulus-response associative chains faithfully adhering to the earlier echo of Thorndike's famous incantation that whatever exists, exists in some amount.

All that the child is, or was, became observable, measurable, and, therefore, capable of experimentation and control in the interests of schooling the young. The distinctions between knowing and saying, being and acting, competence and performance were overlooked in the orgy of mental testing and experimentation that began at the turn of the century and has continued largely unabated since.

The current popularity of child management programs, of P.E.T. and T.E.T.,[46] of classroom management, of behavioral curriculum objectives and outcomes, which pervade the school systems, set in motion an industry of behavioral engineering that has gained ready and uncritical acceptance within school systems. The age of behavior modification is upon us and finds its greatest impact in institutional settings—in prisons; in hospitals; in homes for the autistic, the retarded, and other such powerless populations; for it is within this behavioral paradigm that the image of the child is at its most debased, where a tabula rasa child, able to be controlled and maniplated, is the blueprint for the effective domestication of childhood.

Piaget and His Stage Theory Descendants

Piaget's observational work with children in natural settings has greatly contributed to our insights about the different social space that children occupy. Young children do see the world differently from adults and restructure their experiences accordingly. While Piaget's invariant stage theory (from the sensorimotor period of infancy to the formal operations of adolescence and beyond) may rightly be criticized as culture-bound and hierarchically rigid, his work is important in that he has allowed his subjects, the children, to define their world, and it is their perceptions of reality which have informed his subsequent epistemology of children's cognition.

Unfortunately, it is precisely those characteristics of Piaget's epistemological framework that are the most flawed by his endeavors to create a "scientific" theory of childhood (as opposed to his observational insights, which are illuminating), that have been seized upon by educators and psychologists alike and frozen into prepackaged hypotheses about cognitive developmental stages, moral development, moral reasoning, and even moral education.

Lawrence Kohlberg,[47] who seems to have the last expert word at present on the moral development of children, has constructed an elaborate hierarchy of moral stages from the premoral orientation of "punishment and obedience" followed by "naive instrumental hedonism" to a so-called "morality of individual principles of conscience (sixth stage!)." The authority from which Kohlberg claims to have derived this cross-cultural set of moral-cognitive universals is based on hypothetical moral dilemmas presented to children of all ages in the United States and various other cultures. Here, morality is abstracted out of the immediacy of significant context (e.g., should a husband steal a drug to save a dying wife?) and the typology used to categorize children's judgments bears no relation to the distinctively different experiences of culture class and political-economic structure in which the children are participants. Further, the adult-defined stages of moral reasoning are irrelevant to the very real ethical struggles and dilemmas that children and other people experience in times of crisis.

It is the children in Robert Coles's five-volume *Children of Crisis* who really show us the nature of childhood thinking, the moral sensitivity and intense struggle, the Rubys of the deep South,[48] the Peters of the migrant camps,[49] and even the Larrys of the very wealthy[50] who speak for the moral sensibilities of the child, which are not inferior or in a lesser stage of "development" any more than those of some adults. Rather, we find a sense of morality born of concrete involvement in the world, as distinct from the answers to the vacuous questions detached from existential reality that our social scientists have created in "objective" distance from the ground of social and personal struggle. It is appropriate, therefore, that Coles, in speaking about "children as moral observers," should ask,

> Do we really need a so-called "expert" parading his years of "research" with various American children of different sorts (with respect to age, racial or social or regional background) to tell us what has been appreciated over and over

again by parents and grandparents and older brothers and sisters and schoolteachers and Scout leaders and athletic coaches and ministers and doctors and nurses—by anyone who has occasion to have a talk or two with a child...? Do we really need, more precisely, yet another of our secular "authorities" to tell us that children, young children, indeed, definitely do possess a moral sensibility, an increasingly well muscled notion of right and wrong, and yes, a yearning that justice be done?[51]

Do we really need, then, the research of Hoffman and others,[52] who make their careers from measuring the empathy capabilities of children, defined in the language of experimentation and verification, of assessing the impact of conditioning and empathic arousal, of the relation between discipline and moral development when, in fact, the children about whom these detached "behavioral investigators" claim to speak are no longer there; they are the "invisible men" of Ralph Ellison, about whom and upon whom stages are imposed, consciousness typologized, and grant proposals funded. They are the new commodities in a fast-growing "science" of ethics about which is developing the new industry of morality. No wonder, then, images of contemporary childhood are shackled in the laboratories of our "new breed of experts creating a malignant self consciousness."[53]

In summary, we see how the idea of childhood has been transformed and reconstituted in successive historical eras—from the widespread brutality of antiquity to the miniature adultism of the medieval period and, later, to the creation of the industrial child-workers who were judged psychologically competent at the age of seven or eight, and considered able to take care of themselves and younger siblings. But today, having separated children from the world of work, having infantilized their perceptions and moral sensibilities with insidious moral inventories and taxonomies, having circumscribed their lives in schooling institutions where their experiences, intellect, and state of being are constantly measured, quantified, and evaluated, we have perhaps rediscovered childhood, but in so doing eroded its very ontology as a life phase.

Understanding the Child's Experiences of the World

How, then, do we come to understand the child's experiences? If social science has produced an image of childhood that is alienated from the ground, the very being of child life, how do we ensure a return "to the things themselves"?

Perhaps it is necessary to become anthropologists of childhood, recognizing that we are both embedded in, and yet distanced from, that very culture we once inhabited.

The hermeneutic task that such a commitment engenders engages the researcher in a quest for meaning and understanding which Hans Georg Gadamer has described as a "fusion of horizons."[54] Inasmuch as hermeneutics involves the encountering of meanings not immediately understandable, meanings that require interpretive effort, it is the task of the adult "researcher" to uncover the existential ground of the everyday life experiences of the child and render them visible to those in power by giving them sensible actuality.

Human action is imbued with inexhaustible possibilities of meaning which fill the world in which the child exists, and which she encounters in the course of growing up. It is this personal history that the child shapes through the meanings that she assigns to her experience, to the beckoning world which is an invitation to her to become a meaning-maker. We must attempt to understand that structuring of meaning, for only then can we hope to understand the meaning and consciousness of childhood. In the words of Dutch phenomenologist F. J. Buytendijk, the child is not "something with characteristics, but an initiative of relationships to a world where he chooses and by which he is chosen."[55]

How we choose to investigate the meaning and forms of a modern childhood, and the *methods* that we use to understand the everyday lives of children, is the major quest of the following chapter.

2

The Question of Method

Lives as opposed to problems may puzzle the fixed
notions of theorists . . . to approach certain lives, not
to pin them down, not to confine them with labels,
not to limit them with heavily intellectualized
speculations, but again, to approach, to describe, to
transmit as directly and sensibly as possible what
has been seen, heard, grasped, felt by an observer
who is also being constantly observed himself—not
only by himself but by others, who watch and doubt
and fear and resent him, and also, yes, show him
kindness and generosity and tenderness and affection. The aim, once again then, is to approach, then
describe what there is that seems to matter.

Robert Coles
CHILDREN OF CRISIS[1]

What is there "that seems to matter" in children's lives,
specifically in social institutions like schools? What of the special mysteries of very young lives—lives so far away in time
and space from our own—lives that certainly do "puzzle" the
"fixed notions" of our experts? How can we come to understand the meaning and experience of a modern childhood?
These questions direct us back to the children themselves,
demand the renunciation of a mechanistic psychologism and
an instrumental operationalism in order to return to the
ground and being of the culture of childhood.

Becoming an anthropologist of a culture once inhabited, yet
now transcended, involves a dialectical reconciliation with
one's own historicity. As Wordsworth aptly put it, "The child
is father of the man," and we are, ourselves, embodied in this
generational biography of childhood and adulthood.

How then, in this age of "science," do we research the lives of children? Do we adopt the stance of the detached "behavioral investigator," fearing contamination of our "objectivity" through participation in the world of our subjects? Or, do we, in Paulo Freire's words, enter into "a dialogical encounter"[2] with those whose lives we are attempting to understand and portray?

It is perhaps worthwhile at this point to pause and consider these questions and examine the impact of the current unidimensional concept of science upon the lives of children. The contemporary image of childhood has been fashioned and maintained by the institutions of social science, and by a corresponding methodology that is so rooted in the epistemological universe of positivism that "for close to a century now, many psychologists have seemed to suppose that the methods of natural science are totally specifiable, that the applicability of these to social and human events is not only an established fact, but that knowledge based on inquiries not saturated with the iconology of science is worthless."[3]

While historically the contributions to knowledge of a positivist epistemology are unmistakable, severe deficiencies become apparent when this epistemology is translated into *method* and applied to children living in, and inhabiting, not a physical world of matter and immutable biological laws, but a social world ridden with the bewildering complexity of human life itself.

Hence, an attempt needs to be made to uncover the limitations inherent in a positivist epistemology and in its practical translation into a quantitative research methodology.[4] This quantitative lens, through which children's lives are filtered, measured, and thereafter stamped with the legitimating seal of statistical credibility, creates a "cult of the fact,"[5] freezing their experiences under the tyranny of an obdurate objectivity whose mythmaking powers continue to spellbind generations of "childhood scientists," marching to do battle in the white-coated armour of their tribe, there to defend the faith with *rigor, precision,* and *certitude* against the hermeneuts of the human sciences![6]

The results of this struggle, in which the positivist Weltanschauung holds sway, are such that the focus of social science research is frequently directed not to the exploration of the *meaning* of childhood but away from, not toward, a view of the world which embodies the perspective of its actors, i.e., the children. This leads to the creation of theory in alienation from one's child subjects and their landscape of experience. A narrow focus on technique replaces the puzzlement about a child's understanding of the world, and the quantophrenia surrounding method fosters a trained incapacity for critical and penetrating reflection on the lives that lie beyond categories, labels, and the "fixed notions" of theorists.

The Demystification of Science

Science manipulates things and gives up living in
them. It makes its own limited models of things;
operating upon those indices or variables to effect
whatever transformations are permitted by their
definitions, it comes face to face with the real world
only at rare intervals. Science is and always has
been that admirably active, ingenious, and bold way
of thinking whose fundamental bias is to treat
everything as though it were an object in general.[7]

Science, like our theory and knowledge of the world, is the product of a particular set of sociohistorical conditions. If we follow Mannheim,[8] and adopt a sociology of knowledge perspective where no human thought is immune to the ideologizing influences of its social context, we become aware of the relativity of all perspectives on human events and the social situatedness of thought. Science, then, as both theory and method, becomes a social construction of reality, a second-order construct, which itself has become the model of the world which is assumed to represent reality. But is this scientific model the self-representation of the world it is taken to be—or does science, in fact, only come face to face with the real world at rare intervals? If so, we have created an alien image of human self-representation—where the "scientific" idea of childhood pieced together from fragmented atomized components of the child's existential being results in a reductionistic and degraded image of the child, modeled on natural science and emulating the laws of physics with an unquestioned credibility.

The social implications of this degraded image of the child

are far-reaching. In accepting the false dichotomies of science—of thought from action, emotion from reason, subject from object—we reduce the child to a set of isolated functions, capable of being measured and analyzed in separation from other component parts. This atomization has resulted, for example, in a conception of *intelligence* as a unitary quantity, a *product*, not an integrative human action upon reality. (IQ testing mirrors this fallacy, as do the endless series of measures about learning, motivation, derived objectives, mastery scores, etc.)

And if we do not, mercifully, separate the mind and the human affect from each other, we can take another path to what Paulo Freire has called this "focalistic vision"; we can separate the individual from his social milieu, we can analyze the child in isolation from the familiar—from family, from friends, and too, from the context of culture and class—and we can claim, on the basis of our sophisticated questionnaires, to have developed theories of moral judgment or empathy or, better still, scales of self-image and self-actualization! We can separate consciousness from the unconscious and claim oedipal hostility when, for example, young blacks took to the streets in the late sixties, rioting in rage against the injustice and exploitation of their lives![9]

The most salient effect of the "focalistic vision," however, is that when we are conditioned to see only aspects of reality, we are deprived of the possibility of a genuine action on that reality understood in its totality of structural relations. To critically intervene in reality involves seeing the interconnectedness of the personal and social, of class and culture, of history and the present. The child is not a deculturated, isolated monad, existing in ahistorical relationships to his era, but, rather, lives in culture, in language, and makes history together with other human beings. When the task of the "childhood scientist" fails to be an activity embedded in the cultural landscape of the history-making subject but is, instead, a process of reification and distance, a paradigm of social alienation is generated, predicated not on the ontology of intentional child actors, but on the objectification of passive subjects.

The Technological Ideology and Schooling

If we attempt to analyze the thematic universe of the twentieth century, and understand how a blatant technological ideology has come to dominate the educational system in which children are schooled, we realize the further implications of this focalistic, ahistorical vision. Jacques Ellul,[10] writing on the technological order, claims that technology has become the new and specific milieu in which we are required to exist. This milieu has essentially modified the ideas, judgments, beliefs, and values of the human being, resulting in the formation of new myth systems which foster technological expertise and technical culture at the cost of social concern and human development. The linkages between a positivist Weltanschauung, technology seen as a social form, and the detached objective consciousness spawned within this infrastructure, influence not only the major institutions of the culture such as schools but also the actual practice of research with children.

The breeding of a technological consciousness involves the social-psychological organization of specific forms of knowledge which are intrinsic to technological production, requiring of their technical workers a specific cognitive style, which, in turn, becomes part of the popular consciousness. Peter Berger and his colleagues have analyzed the particular characteristics engendered by this cognitive style in an excellent essay entitled "Technological Production and Consciousness."[11] Here they discuss *measurability, componentiality,* the acceptance of *hierarchy,* the *segregated clusters of consciousness, anonymous social relations,* and *emotional management* as required competencies of the technical worker. These social-psychological characteristics effectively carry over from the workplace, and elements of this consciousness are transposed onto social life, creating an overarching symbolic universe into which secondary carriers of this technological consciousness find a congenial home—in research institutions, schools, and universities. This results in a "mode of massification" which in advanced technological societies, claims Freire,[12] occurs through a subtle domestication of one's critical faculties and the anesthetizing of the consciousness of technical man or woman, whereby a functional pragmatism—dedicated to maintaining the current reality and not to transforming the structures of oppression and relations of domination—is fostered by a technological elite. "The way human beings are related to each other in work, and in their community and family life is largely, if not overwhelmingly determined by the nature of the technology employed, how it is employed and the social relations that govern its use."[13]

This blatant technological ideology dominates the theory and practice of education as well as research;[14] for the constant preoccupation in schools is with child "management" problems, behavioral and instructional objectives, tracking, emotional and cognitive assessment scales, standardized testing, cost-benefit analysis, and effectiveness criteria, so that the educational process is reduced to a technical system with measurable input-output variables.

Technology, like research and education, is never neutral but is embedded in an ideological Weltanschauung reflecting one's own embeddedness in a sociopolitical order. It follows, then, that method, technology, and ideology are inextricably woven together in our contemporary thematic universe. It is through this multihued lens that our contemporary "science" of the child must be viewed and so distinguished from the human sciences, whose set of paradigmatic assumptions, commitments, and dialectically juxtaposed themes lead us in different directions along the paths of other possibilities.

Human Science and the Search for Meaning in Childhood

The basic factor of contemporary culture [is] science and its industrial technological utilization . . . Science always stands under definite conditions of methodological abstraction and the successes of modern sciences rest on the fact that other possibilities for questioning are concealed by abstraction . . . Thus what is established by statistics seems to be a language of facts, but which questions these

facts answer and which facts would begin to speak if
other questions were asked are hermeneutical
questions.[15]

The central task of the hermeneutical researcher is the quest
for meaning, for we are "condemned" to be meaning-makers,
and the interpretation of that meaning created in the *lebens-
welt* (life-world) is the focus of hermeneutics in the human
sciences.

Hermeneutics has its origins in breaches of intersubjectivity
where we encounter meanings that are not immediately
understandable, meanings that lie in the domain of self-
representation requiring interpretive effort. Perhaps one of
the most demanding forms that the hermeneutical art presents
us with, is the breach in intersubjective understanding between the child's life-world and that of the adult.

Inasmuch as "understanding is an event, a movement of
history itself in which neither interpreter nor text can be
thought of as autonomous parts,"[16] so too is the act of understanding the child an event and movement in history; neither
adult nor child can be thought of as autonomous parts, for the
historicity of childhood is a fundamentally human historicity.
Thus, interpretation of the child's life-world must involve not
an adult reconstruction of alien events and life forms, not the
methodological alienation of the knower from what is to be
known, but rather a mediation between these two horizons.
Gadamer's concept of understanding as a *fusion of horizons*
engenders an inexhaustible source of possibilities of meaning,
in which both the knower and the to-be-known are transformed in this dialectical interplay of interpretation. "This
process of understanding that culminates in the fusion of horizons has more in common with a dialogue between persons or
with the buoyancy of a game in which the players are absorbed, than it has with the traditional model of a methodo-
logically controlled investigation of an object by a subject."[17]

It follows, then, from this insightful commentary on the nature of understanding that the path to be traveled by the her-
meneuticist of childhood lies in the direction suggested by
Gadamer. We, in the process, become anthropologists of
childhood, investigating the phenomenology of that life project in order to derive insight into the meaning structures

of that life-world *and* to be transformed by our understanding of the experience; for understanding the child from the perspective of his world is to hold the view that, despite biographical and developmental determinants, the growing child *is* an intentional actor constructing a life project with consciousness, that becoming in the world involves a dynamic self-representation,[18] that the child too, is a historical being, a maker of history, a meaning-maker involved in a praxis upon the world.

How, then, does the researcher, engaged in this particular form of the interpretive act, make visible the existential ground of the everyday life experiences of the child—give actuality to the commonplace, which is the very "stuff" of the life phase of childhood?

Descriptions—clear, vivid, faithful descriptions of experiences, of actions, of words, of phenomena—are central to the hermeneutical undertaking. It is here that **phenomenology** as an appropriate approach, rather than "method," becomes apparent. It is an attempt to describe the world of the child through the art of sensitive observation in order

> To let that which shows itself
> Be seen from itself
> In the very way in which
> It shows itself from itself.[19]

The phenomenological task, therefore, lies both in the process of description and critical reflection where the primacy of experience holds sway, and in the attempt to penetrate to the essence of a phenomenon, to the core themes that underlie *what* is being observed. It is the material produced from an intensive participatory field study of situational microcontexts that gives actuality to the macroworld beyond, where "social actions are comments on more than themselves ... [and where] small facts speak to large issues."[20] Following Geertz's formulation of interpretive ethnography, not only description but "thick description" is required, in which the "inscription" of social discourse and action renders the meaning structure visible in concrete context and actuality. It is for this reason that theory so developed must always "hover low" over its grounded actions, over the concreteness of everyday experience played out in specific contexts. The immediacy of this "thick description," Geertz claims, gives us access to the conceptual world beyond which our subjects inhabit but which becomes vacant, devoid of meaning, if divorced from the site and realm of experience and action.

The Research Dialectic

The dialectic is revealed only to an observer
situated inside the system.[21]

Sartre, in his preface to the *Critique of Dialectical Reason*, sheds further light upon the task of the human science researcher engaged in the dialectical act of research. In order to understand human experience, the researcher must insert himself into the landscape of experience, for, argues Sartre, the dialectical method inextricably weaves the researcher and the subject into a landscape of action and co-constitution of meaning. Dialectical reason can, therefore, never take a stance outside of the system to which it must apply itself; for our knowledge derived from the experienced phenomenon is intertwined with our knowledge of the dialectic; it is both a method of knowing and a movement in the object known. Thus, claims Sartre, those who begin their enquiries with facts will never arrive at essences. This "fact gathering" psychology, which Sartre attacks, produces a fragmented perception of reality precisely because the aim is to gather isolated data from isolated parts of the organism. Sartre accuses psychologists of isolating bodily reactions,[22] behavior, and states of consciousness. But such facts, documented and "verified," will never be more than facts among other facts, facts closed in on themselves, not permitting a grasp of the totality of the human gestalt and resulting in the "focalistic vision" that prevents a genuine transforming action on reality.

Research, then, for Sartre and Freire, involves both the dialogical character of interpretation and a critical intervention in reality, for "to understand is to change to go beyond oneself."[23]

It is here that the praxis of a social phenomenology of childhood lies. Understanding alone is not sufficient, nor is a probing of the essence of the everyday life-world of the child; knowledge and understanding must be linked to the social world, grounded in existential praxis. One does not understand the structures of reality without transforming them through the mediation of a critical reflexivity on the part of the researcher, who is also transformed in this process.

Thus, it is necessary to ground social phenomenology in the direct experiences of children. When the description and reconstruction of experiential data have taken place, a critical and reflexive dialectical analysis is made, the search for themes in the internal structure leading to a search for themes in the external structure, so that small-scale, microscopic, situation analysis forms the bridge to the megaworld beyond. As praxis does not reside within the confines of one's consciousness apart from the world, consciousness and the world become simultaneous and *understanding* leads to *change*, to a going beyond oneself, to the transforming nature of "conscientization."[24] It is in this way that research becomes a praxis upon the world. And research into the nature and meaning of childhood becomes a praxis, articulated in full commitment to the life project of the child.

Aesthetics and the Life Project of the Child

Around him is space, to be filled and defined by
movement and gesture; around him is also silence
to be filled with meaning, using words and sounds,
and at moments when all else fails him, including
the words, the silence itself.[25]

Perhaps it is playwrights, such as Athol Fugard, or poets, such as William Blake and Dylan Thomas, who have best understood, through the aesthetic paradigm in which they live and move with acute sensitivity, those quintessential human attributes that capture the elusive and history-making moments of childhood. Fugard, writing of the fundamental dependence of theater on the living actor "commissioned" to be and make of space and silence a world of meaning, could, with these words, equally well have described the life project of the child, whose human "becoming" involves that same dynamic

self-representation and self-interpretation in space and time.
The child's mode of being in the world is such that the world
becomes an invitation. It is things in the beckoning world that
invite the child, that awaken his curiosity, that invoke him to
make sense of the multitude of experiences lying beyond; in
short, to become, through his play, both an actor and a
meaning-maker.

William Blake's *Auguries of Innocence* captures those moments of wonder, encapsulated in the simple gesture, the
single action of a very young child, which any parent or sensitive baby-watcher will recognize:

> To see a World in a Grain of Sand
> And a Heaven in a Wild Flower
> Hold Infinity in the palm of your hand
> And Eternity in an hour.[26]

With that intense and pantheistic imagery Blake seems to
enter into the heart and mind of childhood through his
verse—itself an inscription of the social action and meaning of
a moment in childhood.

Dylan Thomas, in another evocation, depicts the child's
sense of freedom embodied in movement, in color and space,
and the transformative nature of that experience; for it is these
history-making acts of the child which invest everyday life
experiences with consciousness and meaning in the very act of
being.

> About the lilting house and happy as the grass ·
>   was green,
>   The night above the dingle starry,
>   Time let me hail and climb
>   Golden in the heydays of his eyes,
> And honoured among wagons I was prince of the
>   apple towns.[27]

It is this ontology of childhood that seems so sensitively
captured by the aesthetic paradigm, which, in many ways,
offers a far more accurate portrayal of the mode of being of
childhood than the indifferent, technical vocabularies of our
modern era.

How then do we research the enigmatical nature of childhood? And how do we come to understand the lives of some

children in certain institutional settings? We have seen how a mechanistic psychologism and a scientistic, behavioral technology have masked the ontology of childhood. I have suggested that it is to the human sciences and the arts that we must now turn, in order to seek other possibilities for meaning, another explanatory language that speaks to the *landscape of childhood.*

3

Introduction to the Landscape of Childcare

The focus of my discussion will now shift from the broad idea of childhood to a specific *form* of modern-day childhood— played out in the living theater of childcare institutions. In order to explicate the social context of this form of childhood, it is necessary first to present a brief historical overview of the "schooling of childhood" and the ideological metaphors that color our understanding of this landscape.

A Brief Background to the "Schooling" of Childhood

The rise of mass education in the United States after the industrial revolution generally resulted in the shift of influence from the family to the school. School, no longer the preserve of the upper class, evolved rapidly to meet the needs of industrial employers for a disciplined and skilled labor force. The primary function of the school became that of a maintenance institution providing a mechanism for social and political control in the interests of political stability. An ideal preparation for factory and office work was found in the social relations of the school—specifically in its emphasis on discipline, punctuality, acceptance of authority, and accountability for one's work. Social relations in the school replicated in part the social relations of the workplace, fostering the adaptation of the young to the social division of labor—thereby reproducing the class structure that mass education supposedly diminished.[1]

Historically, in fact, argue Cave and Chesler, the schools have always been mediators of political and economic stability

41

and "exist as agents of the larger social, economic and political context. Thus they correspond to and implement the institutions of the larger society by serving the functions assigned to them . . . those of reproducing the social order."[2]

The impact on children who, from kindergarten to high school, spend hours each day in such a maintenance institution has been bitterly attacked and debated by many radical educators and social commentators, whose concern for the existential quality of the lives of children and the meaning and relevance of the education they receive is paramount. Perhaps Jonathan Kozol has been the most damning of critics: "The containment of youth, which lies at the heart of school indoctrination, depends upon the demolition of a child's ideological and ethical perceptions quite as much as psychological obliteration, tedium and torpor . . . School is the ether of our lives by now: the first emaciation along the surgical road that qualifies the young to be effective citizens."[3] What happens when this "containment of youth" becomes the "containment" of infants, toddlers, and the very young? How much greater is the schooling impact when it coincides with an extremely vulnerable life phase of dependency and attachment?

This is the level at which the question of childcare needs to be examined—a level that looks to the "ideologization" of early childhood.[4] Ironically, it is at this level that a radical social philosophy of freedom endorses the early institutionalization of children precisely because another movement for liberation presents itself as the dialectical antithesis to the containment of children—the women's movement. It is at this paradoxical intersection of history that the woman and her child sadly find themselves at war with one another, vying for freedoms denied in the capitalist structure of domination, in which, historically, both have been commodities. How to resolve this dilemma in favor of a full humanization for both women and children is a complex and controversial issue—and one which I will return to in chapter 10.

The task that lies before me now is to familiarize my reader with an overview of the childcare landscape before moving *into* that landscape, there to inhabit and describe the full range of social action that lies within.

Childcare—Past and Present

Daycare[5] in this country dates back well over a century and, in its inceptions and social relations, has mirrored the class structure and social division of labor evident in the schooling system.

The day nursery,[6] which became popular in the United States toward the end of the nineteenth century, was founded to provide care for the children of working mothers. It was modeled on the French and English attempts, the latter led by British philanthropist Robert Owen, who opened the first of the American "infant schools" in Indiana in 1825.

Another day nursery that became prominent during the nineteenth century was the Boston Infant School, whose trustees justified the establishment of this center as follows: "Such a school would be of eminent service . . .; by relieving mothers of a part of their domestic chores, it would enable them to seek employment . . . [and the children] would be removed from the unhappy association of want and vice, and be placed under better influences."[7] This center accepted children between eighteen months and four years, and provided all-day care and a noon lunch. Children were required to be presented clean, washed, and dressed in whole, clean clothes!

The Nursery for the Children of Poor Women was another East Coast day nursery, founded in 1854 by the New York Hospital. Here cleanliness was even further emphasized, and children between six weeks and six years were bathed and dressed in hospital clothes upon arrival, and were cared for by nurses.

The rapid growth of the day nursery in the latter part of the nineteenth century was a response to the severe hardships experienced by mostly single or deserted mothers, not only left to care for their children but forced, out of economic necessity, to work. The day nursery was both a social welfare philanthropic institution and an attempt to "school" the poor in the moral training grounds of the center. As one day nursery worker was reported to remark, "Slum babies would all be better off in nurseries."[8] Furthermore, the social dislocation caused by rapid industrialization and the massive influx of immigrants also brought about the problem of the "acculturation" of the immigrant child living in tenements, unable to speak the language and often left to fend for herself on the streets as mothers and fathers were forced to take whatever work was available. The day nursery thus became the solution to the effective socialization of both the children of the poor and the immigrant poor—a progressive alternative to the orphanage, incarceration, the asylum, and the reformatory; for these latter institutions had previously served as the dumping ground for the casualties of poverty.

Steinfels describes how the day nursery movement captured the imagination of wealthy, upper-class women who expressed great concern for the plight of young, poor, dirty children, neglected and often left to fend for themselves as their mothers went off to the factory or domestic service. "The day nursery ladies are easily enough criticized for their *noblesse oblige*, their condescension, the foisting of their own values on the poor ... Nevertheless, given their limited class interests and narrow experience, these women managed to create the day nursery. In retrospect their creation seems flexible, practical, and above all, genuinely responsive to the needs of working mothers."⁹ This concern for working mothers was an interesting and almost unique posture at the time. The goal of day nurseries was not only to care for the children of the poor but to assist the mothers both in training and employment in a way which, Steinfels implies, was far more progressive than many of our current policies and daycare services.

The Helen Day Nursery in Chicago was one such exemplary center, where a great sensitivity for the work patterns of the neighborhood mothers created a supportive community center of part-time and full-time daycare, in addition to being a social community center, responsive to family crises.

During this same period when the day nursery flourished, the kindergarten movement was introduced by German emigrés, and in 1860 the first such center for English-speaking children was opened by Elizabeth Peabody. The kindergarten, however, was oriented not to custodial care but rather to loftier educational goals. It served a smaller and different population of young children, whose physical and economic needs were met in the family and where the desperate situation of poverty was absent.

The sudden shift in attitudes toward the day nursery from a charitable, philanthropic organization in the 1890s was the result of a change in attitudes caused by the entry into this field of the professional preschool teacher and social worker in the 1920s.

The result was that the day nursery came under close scrutiny by a group whose philosophy and predispositions were unsympathetic to the notion that a mother should work and that a child should be cared for outside his home in a group setting. This attitude differed from that of the early charity workers, who, though they disapproved of working mothers and the group care of children, recognized that necessity dictated that many mothers must work. For them the day nursery was a superior alternative to total institutionalization of the child. The view of the professional social worker came to dominate thinking in the day care field at the same time as it projected an image to the public of the day nursery as a custodial and undesirable service for women and families *who were not normal* [my emphasis].[10]

The era of daycare as an underfinanced, marginal service for the "pathological" poor then followed, coinciding with a depletion of interest by the philanthropists of the upper classes and a growing belief that a mother's place was in the home. This heralded the end of the progressive, innovative ideas of the previous period.

It was not until the emergency mobilization of men and women required by the Second World War that daycare once again, in different forms, came into its own, and prejudice against the working mother gave way to the exigencies of the war effort. By July 1945 more than 1½ million children were in daycare. The end of the war and the changeover to a peacetime economy resulted in the shutting down of thousands of centers and left thousands of mothers (who *did not* give up their jobs after the war), and over a million children, without daycare services.

The prevailing social ideology of a motherhood-at-home, buttressed by the dominant images of Freudian psychology, restored the earlier conception of daycare as a service designed for the poor and pathological family. This view prevailed, even into the sixties. In 1963, the Children's Bureau (H.E.W.) found that "Day care makes it possible for many parents to keep their children with them in their own homes and to retain their legal and financial responsibility. Therefore, day care is a way of strengthening family life, preventing neglect of some children, and reducing risk of separation from their families for others."[11]

The salient themes that emerge from the preceding historical overview are, once again, direct commentaries on the relations between mothers and their children, and on a body of professionals and legislators who, at whim and in accord with changing and often expedient social ideologies of the poor and of children, create, break, and resurrect childcare programs and services for working women.

Perhaps the strongest influence on the situation of daycare in modern times has been the women's movement. In keeping with the demythologization of the "feminine mystique," with the changing role of women and their reentry into the economy, particularly in the middle classes, women began to demand daycare as a civil right. In the last decade, the image of daycare has shifted from that of a privilege provided for the poor to a necessary service both for women who have to work and for those who *choose* to work, to follow a career, or to pursue higher education.

In addition, this same era of women's liberation and the demand for full-time daycare services has also seen the rapid growth of part-day nursery schools with cognitive-based preschool curricula to meet the aspirations of a largely middle-class population, desiring to provide their children with "readiness" training in preparation for their entry into kindergarten. There has also been an increased emphasis on the advantages of early education intervention programs for lower-income children, whom experts have seen fit to label "culturally deprived," and the establishment of Head Start programs.

In summary, then, we have viewed a fundamental change in attitude toward daycare.

Among the demands around which the women's movement originally gathered, day care, free and universally available, was seen as a key element in allowing women to pursue careers on an equal basis with men. The women's movement served to unite the long standing needs of working mothers who, in the late forties, the fifties, and sixties worked because of economic need, with the more recent movement of middle- and upper-class women away from total involvement in child-rearing and toward the pursuit of employment and careers for reasons of self-fulfillment.[12]

Daycare: Yes or No—the Great Ideological Debate

Daycare of the seventies and the eighties has become the ideological battleground where the controversial social issues of the last decade have been played out. The children, caught powerless on the periphery of this class and gender fray, are nevertheless tossed back and forth by the changing currents of the time.

The demand for free and universally available daycare from birth onward is a women's issue rather than a child issue, and we need to acknowledge that honestly. This demand has, inherent in it, many complex problems which are central to the being of the developing child but which, in a capitalist system, pit not only worker against owner but the rising "class" of women against their own children. It is a fight for rights—and a bitter one—as the mother, unwittingly in most cases, prepares for war against her child, and the price of female liberation is bought at the dialectically opposed cost of the oft-eroded freedom of one's children. Free and universally available daycare is a simplistic catch phrase and, like all revolutionary slogans, needs demystification. It is fraught with a complex set of questions and resulting ambiguities: What kind of daycare? Do we include all ages of children from infancy? Who will fund and control the centers—the federal government, churches, factories, companies, private franchises? Will this result in Kate Millet's professionalization of childhood? What about parent participation? Where will these centers be based—in neighborhoods, the workplace, professional or executive corporations? Will this free and universally available daycare be modeled on our current schooling system? If so, what of the "containment" phenomenon that Kozol so bitterly attacks? Furthermore, is this demand for free and uni-

versal daycare a middle-class demand or is it shared by working women of the poor? Or would other options such as a
guaranteed income be the preference of those who are poor,
for whom childcare is yet another burden? These and many
other complex issues need to be critically analyzed before the
institutionalization of all young children, from infancy through
preschool, is so readily advocated. In addition, other cross-
cultural models of childcare (such as those found in Israel,
Sweden, China, Cuba, and certain African societies), while
problematical in their own right, are often more sensitive and
humane than our own disarray of alternatives and need to be
discussed. I shall return to the conflict of freedoms between
women and their children and possible alternatives in chapter
10.

Daycare and Attachment

The most compelling arguments against daycare for young
children emanate from those in the mental health field who
stress the importance of an intense primary attachment to a
mother or mother substitute. Bowlby's well-known research
on infant attachment and maternal deprivation *is* important,[13]
yet, unfortunately, has been seized upon by both feminists
and anti-daycare proponents alike, and distorted out of its
original context. Bowlby has been vilified as a male chauvinist
supporting the continued oppression of women shackled to
households swarming with infants, and has been alternately
lauded as the high priest of mother-infant love, and the advocate of a traditional motherhood. Neither of these is a useful or
accurate interpretation of a theory which, it should be re-
membered, was grounded in studies of babies who suffered
from extreme and prolonged separation from their mothers—a
different experience, indeed, from that of a young child who,
on a regular basis, undergoes a *temporary* separation from a
parent in centers which, in some cases, do provide nurturant
mother-substitutes. Likewise, René Spitz's case study "Hospitalism" documents how babies raised in an impersonal
foundling home but cared for in immaculate and hygenic conditions died or suffered severe retardation in an institutional

environment devoid of human love and warmth.[14] However, this study, and others like it, are not an accurate metaphor for daycare, for daycare is a partial, not a total, institutionalization experience, where children have contact with both care givers *and* parents as part of their everyday life-world.

Hence, while maternal deprivation theory should not be the lens through which the temporary separation of the child in daycare is viewed, it is important to consider the seemingly universal need for early human bonding in a stable, ongoing relationship with a mother or father who really *loves* the child. The lack of this unconditional love results in what Selma Fraiberg has termed "the diseases of non-attachment [which] can be eradicated at the source, by ensuring stable human partnerships for every baby. If we take the evidence seriously we must look upon a baby deprived of human partners as a baby in deadly peril. This is a baby who is being robbed of his humanity."[15] These "diseases of non-attachment," which are, too often, caused by the breaking of primary, early attachment bonds that need to be tended and cultivated from the moment of birth, have far-reaching implications for a future culture of nonattached, unbonded adults, whose ability to form long-lasting, enduring partnerships and friendships, characterized by what Buber has termed "I-Thou," rather than "I-it," relationships, is in jeopardy.

The question to be posed, therefore, when we consider the issue of nonattachment, concerns the capacity of an institutional setting to provide nurturing parent substitutes to which the young can *attach* themselves during the temporary and partial separation from a parent. The Tremont Street Infant Center set up by Jerome Kagan and fellow researchers is an example of an unusually sensitive institution specifically designed to cater to the special needs and vulnerabilities of very young children.[16] Undoubtedly, other such exemplary centers do exist,[17] but Fraiberg's critique, while somewhat one-sided in perspective, does need to be taken seriously. Her position has been attacked by feminists and daycare advocates alike; nevertheless, her account is, sadly, an accurate depiction of the experiences of many children in this country. "When a child spends 11 to 12 hours of his waking day in the care of indifferent custodians, no parent and no educator can

say that the child's development is being promoted or enhanced, and common sense tells us that children are harmed
by indifference."[18]

Clearly, once we begin to explore this complex issue of
attachment, we become aware of the necessity for discussing
children's institutional experiences in the context of their developmental lives. A baby of a year or less is far more vulnerable to the disease of nonattachment than an older toddler; and a
three- or four-year-old, in turn, can handle separation from a
familiar loved one with far more aplomb than a younger child.
This consideration has led to the two-and-a-half- or three-year
fixed aged entrance of many nursery school and daycare centers and to licensing guidelines which supposedly take these
different developmental needs into account. Even given such
requirements, does the specter of nonattachment still haunt
us? Do the shifting staff and overcrowded classes of many
profit-run centers still present a psychological climate of indifference?

These and other questions that focus on the quality of the
child's life in such places can only be answered by an insider's
view of the *social life within,* for by looking long and hard at
the microcosmic world that lies beyond the ideological battleground of daycare, and beyond the theory of early child development and mental health, perhaps our perception of this
phenomenon will be broadened—and we will begin to understand the full implications of creating age-segregated institutions to care for the young. "Brick by brick we are building an American society in which large numbers of infants and
children will be raised in daycare centers. The consequences
of this daily family exodus in which *everyone* leaves home are
as yet unknown."[19] Though unknown, these consequences are
not always negative as Glickman and Springer's words imply.
When we consider the theoretical pros and cons of the daycare argument, we must remember that to find answers to
these questions, we need to return to "the things themselves,"
the everyday lives of the children as *they* experience their
institutional world.

As I prepare to take the reader on an extended visit into
various worlds of experience of the child, I offer a brief sketch

of the larger setting which these centers represent as a prelude to my case-study portraits of childcare institutions.

The National Daycare Picture

There are not many available reports on the condition of daycare in this country. The notable exceptions are Mary Keyserling's *Windows on Daycare,* an extensive survey of hundreds of centers and daycare homes across the nation;[20] and Margaret O'Brien Steinfel's comprehensive discussion of daycare both in its historical and contemporary social context.[21] In addition, the Abt Associates' studies and the reports of the National Center for Education Statistics detail currently available demographic information in the area of daycare.

According to the Keyserling report, which was published in 1972, six million children under the age of six had working mothers, and one million of those children whose mothers worked were living in poverty; yet another million lived in families close to the poverty line. Only a very small percentage of children whose mothers worked benefited from developmental daycare, and well under ten percent were enrolled in licensed daycare. Investigators from the study project noted that three-fourths of the daycare centers were largely segregated institutions serving predominantly white or black populations. Furthermore, in 1970, licensed proprietary (profit-run) and nonprofit centers had an enrollment capacity for 625,000 children, many of whom were cared for part-day. Of the profit-run centers, rated on a scale of "superior," "good," "fair," or "poor," only 1% were evaluated as "superior," 15% as "good," 35% as "fair" (rendering custodial care), and over 50% were evaluated as providing "poor," in some cases abusive, care. Of the nonprofit centers visited, 15% were Head Start programs, and these tended to elicit the highest praise. In the nonprofit centers, 10% were regarded as "superior;" 25%+, "good;" 50%, "fair" (providing only adequate custodial care); and 10%+ as "poor," including some that needed to be shut down.

All in all, researchers visited 431 centers across the country accommodating some 24,000 children. Among highlights of Keyserling's recommendations were:

That comprehensive developmental daycare should be available to all families who wished their children to benefit from such services.

Daycare should be provided without charge for children in low-income families, with fees scaled to income for others.

Daycare should not be regarded as a "welfare" service, but as needed by families at all income levels. All publicly assisted daycare should be integrated racially, ethnically, and socioeconomically.

Furthermore, following the report's findings regarding the acute shortage of adequate daycare facilities for children of working mothers, Keyserling was led to characterize the situation as a "national daycare crisis" in 1972.[22]

Almost a decade later, despite the accelerated number of women entering the work force and the rapidly increasing population of preschool children, we note that the "national daycare crisis" is far from over. Demographic data from the National Institute of Education indicate that only *half* of the nation's three- and four-year-old children are now enrolled in some form of daycare or nursery program.[23] The exact breakdown of numbers within the different types of center offerings is as follows (my own paraphrase of extracts from the report):

Forty percent of daycare centers operated for profit and most of these were run independently of any sponsoring agency. Nonprofit daycare centers were most often sponsored either by churches, the community or the federal government [see bar chart]. Of these 18,300 centers, approximately 900,000 children were served between 1976 and 1977. While the Head Start program represents only a section of the daycare picture, it has served an average of 400,000 preschool children from low-income families each year since its inception in 1965. In addition, another 2.6 million children are enrolled in kindergarten and nursery school programs which are run by the public school system and are usually part-time in structure.

Costs per daycare center ranged from $19 to $25 per week, with costs per child averaging $1,230 in profit-run centers

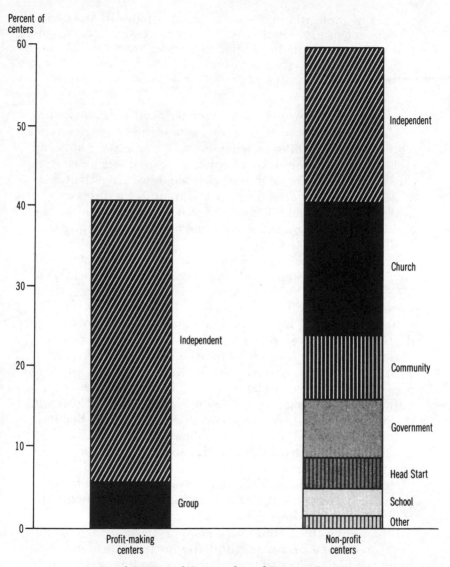

Legal Status and Sponsorship of Daycare Centers.
From Nancy B. Dearman and Valena White Plisko,
The Condition of Education (Washington, D.C.:
National Center for Educational Statistics, 1980).

and $2190 in publicly-funded, nonprofit programs; the
latter have a lower adult-child ratio of 1:5.5 compared to

1:7.5 in profit-run centers. It was also found that salaries were consistently higher, staff education superior, and in-service training more adequate in funded nonprofit daycare programs; once again confirming Keyserling's findings on the qualitative differences between profit and non-profit daycare centers.

In summary, then, on the one hand we have a dismal picture of a daycare crisis in the nation, where the acute needs of working mothers, most of whom *have* to work, are not being met by the provision of an adequate system of organized daycare for their children. On the other hand, we have the words of Selma Fraiberg directing our attention to the problems of profit-run centers and warning us that "the costs paid by the children who are in storage have not been calculated by anyone"![24]

At this point it becomes appropriate to open the "windows on daycare" and step inside and live there for a while, to breathe the air of this microcosmic landscape where "small facts speak to large issues."[25]

In the following five chapters I describe and represent for the reader the lives of children observed over a two-year period in different institutional settings in the American Midwest. I did not consciously choose the best or the worst of these settings to study; and most, according to the criteria ratings of Keyserling, would be considered "good." However, the picture that emerges, when one looks at the lives that hide behind criteria and evaluation categories, is a somewhat different and interesting story of the schooling of our young. These centers represent a slice of life of the national daycare picture—but the issues, complexities, and nuances of the children's lives played out in these settings may illuminate the larger daycare landscape.

While Keyserling, Steinfels, and others have given us useful "snapshots" of the daycare world, it is my purpose to present a finely etched, composite portrait of a modern institutional childhood.[26] This study is grounded in an involvement with eight preschools, in five of which I spent intense periods of observation. In the interest of preserving anonymity I have changed identifying characteristics without distorting the reality of the experience. Like Coles, "Often I have drawn composite pictures: that is, I have combined two or three people (or, centers) in order to make the particular individuals I know unrecognizable and also to emphasize and highlight the issues for the reader."[27] My approach while observing and playing with the children in these centers was to write down, when possible, dialogue and interactions as they occurred, or immediately afterward, using the anthropological license to reconstruct the day's events. In all, I have tried to be faithful to the words and gestures of my subjects.

What follows is an account of my two-year involvement with the children and staff of five case-type centers in the Midwest. Thereafter, having grounded the quest for the meaning of childhood in "thick descriptions" of specific social contexts, I move to an interpretive ethnography of the *idea of childhood*.

2

4

Golda Meir Nursery School

Golda Meir Nursery School is housed in a spacious Jewish community center which is located in a quiet, attractive, residential neighborhood adjacent to a park. The nursery school caters to a predominantly professional group of middle- and upper-income families. While some of the mothers work part-time or are taking graduate degrees, the majority do not work outside the home. Most of the children are brought to the center by their mothers in the morning and picked up again before lunch. It appears that the women, in fairly traditional fashion, assume the major responsibility for childrearing and various after-school arrangements when necessary.

The nursery school offers a part-day program for three-, four-, and five-year-olds, supervised by a female director and head teacher and several licensed preschool teachers who, in turn, are responsible to a board of parents and community members. The center describes its goals as dedicated to the fostering of Jewish cultural awareness, a knowledge of Judaism, and happy, socially adjusted children who are able to gain both social and cognitive skills in readiness for entry into kindergarten and elementary school.

Lived-Time and Institutional Time

The cultural configuration of time demands our
submission, it requires that we renounce impulses
that interfere with it. This is the austerity of time ...
Although most people in our culture restrain the
desire to wander from the compelling path of time,
they are naturally unaware of the enormous amount
of training they need as children to prevent them
from doing so.[1]

59

One of the striking characteristics of this center's program was its rigid adherence to a time schedule to which all activity and play was subordinated. The morning was temporally mapped by the teachers and defined both the spatial and interpersonal modes of existence of the children. The children, in turn, appeared to restructure their experiences accordingly.

> After snacktime, at which orange juice and cookies were served, the children split up into two voluntary groups in anticipation of the story time activity. I overheard Sandra telling a friend, "My mother's coming back soon—right after snack time and story time."

> During my third visit to the school, I was playing with Jerry in the basement. He went up to the director in the midst of our play and asked, "Is it clean-up time yet?" to which Sally, the director, replied, "No, it's not clean-up time yet." A few minutes later, Teacher Lesley called out, "Well, we must get ready to put away blocks—it's clean-up time." As she announced that I thought, "Oh, it must be 9:15," and looked at the clock, which indeed displayed two minutes to 9:15!

Jerry's anticipation of "clean-up time" was analogous to my own response. He could not "tell time," but his sense of time was determined by a schedule which demarcated spatially selected activities to be performed within certain time frames. I, too, upon my third visit, had already internalized the compartmentalization of the day's experiences and associated that with "clock time."

> During a winter visit, Perry came in to one of the classrooms and asked Teacher Lesley, "When is it going to be snack time?" Teacher Lesley proceeded to outline the schedule. "Well, in about fifteen minutes, it will be clean-up time, then snack time and story time and songs, and then go-home time." Perry walked off, apparently satisfied with the answer. A few minutes later he returned to Teacher Lesley and saw children playing a game and asked, "Don't we do *games after songs?*"

> Samantha approached Teacher Sally and said she was hungry. Teacher Sally looked at her watch and said, "It's not hungry time yet"!

At 10:45, the teachers announced, "Time to clean up, guys" in both classrooms. One child promptly got up and carried his drawing to his bag, one among many lining the classroom corridor, and deposited the unfinished drawing in the correctly identified bag. Some children were less willing to get up, but there did not seem to be any extra time given for completing the activity. Teacher Lesley: "We have to clean up now; put the hammer where it belongs, and you can go downstairs if you clean up here."

The concept of allowing a child to complete an activity he was engaged in was subordinate to the compelling nature of the *schedule*, which the teachers planned in advance of the children's experiences. Although engagement in an activity was strongly encouraged, the conflict between the teacher's superimposed time schedule and the experience of the children's "lived time" was striking.

The well-organized, efficient, smooth functioning program depended on a "structured" day. A "structured" day, in turn, meant the breakdown of the morning into a set of component activities which, according to the staff, incorporated a balance of "free play" and "cognitive" learning. The strict demarcation of the morning, by its very organization, denied the children the possibility of a continuous, uninterrupted activity brought to its own natural closure. Instead, the structure was believed efficient by the staff (which indeed it was) and was intended to give the children a sense of security and consistency.

While the children did appear to derive security from the *temporal rigidity*, they clearly became dependent on the structure and felt uncomfortable with any deviation, as we see from the preceding observations. The dependence on structural rigidity appeared to extend to other patterns of behavior, such as a dependence on teacher presence and authority, within certain temporal frames.

During story time (a time when a teacher is always present and in control), the telephone rang and the teacher left the room to answer it. The children looked around and became visibly upset. Mary: "Hey, we don't have no teacher." Seth: "Where is she?" Grant (pointing to me): "Look at her; she's a teacher." Gary: "No, she's not, she's here with a friend."

Mary: "But we need a teacher." Chorus of all four: "We need a teacher."

The children's sense of "planned time" was disturbed by external demands on the teacher, and they were at a loss. They did not speak to each other about the story, or choose to look at the book, or wander around the room. Instead, they expressed their concern about the *loss* of a teacher, who represented both "teacher authority" and "time controller."

The children were not the only ones in this environment who manifested this dependence on planned time. The teachers, having devised a particular series of activities according to time, accordingly became time-dependent.

During almost every visit that I made to this nursery school, there was a consistent pattern of interference by staff in "free-play" time, whereas during cognitive activities the teachers frequently let the children alone. This free-play "hovering syndrome" appeared in the basement when the children were engaged in "play" (climbing, running, riding, building, fantasy, etc.) which did not include the teachers. The teachers appeared at a loss for action and continually hovered over the children, interfering in their play.

> During a number of visits when a certain climbing apparatus was not being utilized, teachers would ask questions like, "Do you want to go on the slide?" "Do you|need something to do?" The children would ignore the teachers and seemed to want to play with their peers rather than with the teachers.

> Brett took three firehats. Teacher Sally: "Do you need three firehats, Brett? What are you going to play?" Brett did not reply but was joined by two other boys, who moved in the direction of the large climbing blocks. The three played "fire engines," and one handed Sandra a firehat as she approached them. She rejected it without producing any apparent reaction on the part of the other child. Teacher Lesley, watching nearby, immediately intervened: "Maybe she doesn't want it; maybe Aaron does."

The teachers were not participants in the children's spontaneous games, neither could they be teachers; hence, they attempted to adopt the role of overseer or supervisor, or to reinstill the cognitive into "free play." When a child was coming down a slide or playing with a boat, they would ask, "Good, what color is the slide?" or "What shape is the boat?"

Although this period was labeled "free play," the children were not *free to play*, nor were they free *not to play*. Engagement in an activity was considered a positive phenomenon by the staff; hence, children who did not play busily were considered to be problematical and in need of help.

Eli stood by the door watching Teacher Sally. Teacher Sally told her three or four times, "Go and play." Eli didn't respond. After the fourth time, Teacher Sally took her by the hand and took her to the kitchen area. "Go and play over there."

Teacher Lesley walked into the basement leading Sharon by the hand. "Why don't you play with Annette on the blocks," she said, and walked off. All three girls stood there, *not playing*. Teacher Lesley appeared anxious and went off to set up a band, with musical instruments for the girls.

Myron stood alone in a corner, sucking his fingers. Teacher Sally came up and asked solicitously, "What are you doing?" She noticed that the child was holding a block. "Oh, you found a block, very good. Let's see where it goes," and led him off and attempted to engage him in a building activity.

Engagement and task involvement were constantly reinforced by the staff, often to absurd extremes. Myron, for example, had clearly displayed no enterprise in "finding" a block; nor did he seem particularly interested in building with the block.

On another occasion I observed Myron standing adjacent to a wooden wagon. Teacher Sally went up to him and said, "That's a nice toy to play with; that's a good idea." Myron was not playing *with* the toy, nor did he after Teacher Sally's remark, but walked off in the direction of the fantasy play area, where he appeared to spend much of his time.

After I had been visiting this center for about three months, I was asked to work there one day at the request of the director, who planned an out-of-town visit. In the role of *teacher* rather than *observer*, I was instructed to "always check that the children have something to do—that they're involved." I was also expected to watch over the children when they played on the slide or on the large climbing blocks in the basement.

The stated concern with safety in the free play area appeared somewhat uncalled for. The children were well developed, competent, physically adept, and extremely familiar with the large-motor apparatus. In addition, the slide was low and bounded by a foam mat, and none of the children encountered any problems in manipulating the climbing blocks. I began to interpret this safety concern as an anxious reaction on the part of the staff, an attempt to monitor that which was free-flowing and unstructured. To impose a manifest structure on "free play" would be too blatant an educational contradiction, but a latent structure masked by the legitimate concern for safety effectively converted "free play" into "controlled" play in a manner that was socially acceptable to the staff. The teachers' desire to intervene was evident both in their "engagement" anxiety and in their overconcern about safety.

These observations led me to a serious consideration of the meaning of *time* for the children in such a preschool institution.

The Function of Organized Time

The Golda Meir Nursery School reflected in large part the cultural configurations of time in an industrialized Western technocracy. In order to "succeed," it is necessary to organize one's life according to an efficient time plan. The vocabulary of cost-benefit analyses, maximum productivity, minimum time wastage, schedules, programmed instruction, behavioral objective modules—all express an attempt to refashion one's lived-time world into the metacategories of institutional time. The fragmentation of one's lived day into a series of appointments and preplanned experiences allows the individual to predict and control, which, in turn, facilitates a technical pragmatism geared to *organization* and *structure*. Hence, to separate time out of our lived existence, imparting to it a sense of objectivity, allows us to become both the controllers and the victims of time. Time is not experienced as a spontaneous part of the lived world but rather as an external force. We speak of "measuring time," the "pressures of time," the "constraints of time," "fleeting time," and "telling time." We expect people to perform certain behavioral and cognitive feats within a measured time period. The ability to perform speedily within a given time frame is prized as a valuable attribute. The defining vocabularies of successful structure and organization are always located within a temporal frame.

Hence, the nursery school's practices are congruent with those of the larger technical culture; it is involved in the active *socialization of institutional time*. The preschool mirrors the temporal organization of the larger system and provides its own temporal interiorization which the children internalize in order to function adaptively.

The Interiorization of Time

Within this structure, the teachers are the "time controllers," the timekeepers of all play. The temporal configurations, in turn, denote the spatial and interactive modes of existence: children may free play in the basement until 9:15; snack time occurs upstairs at 10:15. Outside play is permitted after 10:30. Children may interact "freely" in the basement, but must separate upstairs. Conflict occurs most often during free play time and rarely during snack time. Play is subordinate to, not a part of, time. Bringing a natural closure to an activity is not possible if the temporal boundaries are traversed. Children need to be busy, i.e., "use their time well," but engagement is limited by schedule priorities. The teachers, uneasy with free play time, attempt to make the children more "productive," which augments the sense of sound organization and effective programming.

The children, in adapting to this norm, restructure their world accordingly. The day is divided into different "times": snack time, story time, going-home time, etc., which lends a security and consistency to their morning and facilitates a dependence on teacher authority to control their experiences. The schedule is a rigid one, and I saw no flexibility. One need question whether the internalization of this structural rigidity creates other forms of rigidity in the child—for if his world is not neatly planned and packaged, how does he handle disruptions, deviations from the norm?

The children, in *adapting* to this structure, were clearly being socialized to view the world as stable and secure; experiences were predictable occurrences that fell along a clearly defined continuum. The routinization of activity was stressed, and the novel was relegated to the realm of the disruptive, as exemplified by staff unwillingness to deviate from the schedule upon spontaneous requests by the children.

> One spring morning a request by Kelly to go on a leaf walk was refused by Teacher Sally on the basis of inadequate preparation and other preplanned activities.

Lived-Time

Time is not a line but a network of intentionalities.[2]

In this environment, the children's own experience of lived-time is systematically imposed upon by institutional constraints; hence, creating a dichotomy between the natural lived-time experience and the exigencies of "school" time.

Merleau-Ponty describes time as a presence, an abode, which we, as "body-beings" in the world, inhabit. As such, we, through our intentionality, constitute time; time arises out of our relation with things, and it is we who constitute that relationship. Authentic time is not a continuum, a progressive seriation; and we cannot talk of time apart from our consciousness. We are beings-in-time. Time has no objectivity apart from the body-as-being-in-the-world.

While our primordial experience of lived-time occurs in childhood, as depicted so vividly in Dylan Thomas's "Fern Hill," we should question whether this primordial contact with lived-time is not systematically eroded by the active socialization of institutional time in these young children.

Protectiveness, Warmth, and Praise

The warmth and care in this environment was a striking first
impression, borne out by subsequent visits. The children were
open and friendly to me, even upon my initial entry. During
the morning I worked there as "teacher," they accepted my
authority and status without question and welcomed my
presence. Children were treated benevolently by the staff,
who constantly praised and reinforced effort and endeavor and
were very protective toward them.

> Michael fell off one of the climbing blocks, knocking his
> knee, and picked himself up, not crying. Teacher Anne
> swiftly walked over, followed by Teacher Lesley inquiring
> solicitously about his knee. Michael began to cry and was
> comforted.

> Bradley climbed over a blockade of blocks approximately
> three feet from the floor. Teacher Sally: "That's really not
> a good place to climb. Those blocks are insecure and you
> might fall down."

Entrances assumed an important ritualistic quality each
morning as the children arrived. The teachers always stood by
the door, greeting each child upon entry and frequently
commenting upon appearance.

> Teacher Lesley remarked to Jimmy, as his mother walked
> in holding him by the hand, "Oh, you have *new* shoes on.
> Where did you get them?"

> Teacher Sally admired Sandra's dress. "How pretty." And
> Sandra, in turn, complimented Teacher Lesley on her *new*
> skirt.

Many passing remarks were directed to the "newness" of
clothes, a change in hairstyle, or other facets of appearance.
The children were invariably well dressed, neat, and clean.
They did not wear *old* clothes to school. Evidently the parents
did not anticipate their children engaging in "rough" or
"muddy" play while there.

While the staff were always in readiness to warmly welcome
the arriving children, the mothers of the younger children frequently appeared to emphasize "departure time."

Three-year-old Neil's mother walked into the basement with him, holding his hand. She hugged him three times, and Neil ran off in the direction of the slide. Mother stood there watching and then walked up to the slide and kissed him again. He began to whine and cling to her, followed her out to the door until Teacher Lesley picked him up. As soon as his mother had left, Neil ran back to the slide.

Shane (three years old) and his mother walked into the entrance hall. Shane was whining and holding onto his mother. Mother told him to "Go and play." Shane cried. Mother patted him, comforted him, and prepared to leave. As she was leaving, Shane cried afresh. Mother walked back and blew him a kiss. Teacher Lesley picked him up and carried him over to the band area. He stopped crying immediately.

During the fall, two new little girls entered the three-year-old group. Both mothers would stand outside the basement door, watching the girls (who were friends) and would periodically enter the room whenever the girls cried. On one occasion, Debra cried almost the entire morning, the crying apparently precipitated by each fresh glance of her mother. Both mothers stayed in the school building for two weeks—standing in the corridor when the girls were upstairs.

It appeared that the mothers suffered from "separation anxiety" more severely than their children, and that they, in fact, actively fostered dependence in their offspring by prolonged leavetaking, hovering, and reluctance to part with their children. The children, in turn, appropriately "acted up" (as the teachers termed it) when the mothers were present, and trotted off quite happily when the parents were absent. The teachers then adopted the role of "surrogate" parent and extended to the children the same protectiveness meted out by the parents.

In all aspects, then, there was a sense of security about the environment, evident in the teacher attitudes, the consistency of the schedule, the cohesive planning of activities, and the efficient organization of space and materials.

The cognitive curriculum was planned in advance, and all materials were laid out in readiness for the children before the day began. This preparation tended to prevent object-conflict between children as there was no scarcity of resources.

> When Amy went to paint on the other side of Karen's easel, there was an exact replication of Amy's three jars of colored paint as well as a painting smock available. Two other prepared double easels stood adjacent.

No conflict arose over the easels or the colors; there were many jars of paint, sufficient aprons, and a variety of paint-brushes. The abundance of available resources tended to facilitate a calm rather than conflictful atmosphere during classroom time. Very rarely was it necessary for a child to "take turns" and delay an immediate gratification of needs. I frequently was amazed by the sense of calm and often found myself wondering what those children were like at home. Often I experienced the day as boring, too peaceful, too well paced. At times, however, this was a welcome relief from some other centers I visited.

Whenever the children were successful in their attempts, the teachers would immediately praise them. The vocabulary of "good," "pretty," "well done," was indicative of staff attitudes toward the children which comprised warmth, interest, attentiveness, and concern about the need for continual activity engagement.

> Cyndy put on a plastic apron by herself before playing at the water table. Teacher Judy: "That was real good, Cyndy."

> Myron set out a fantasy table of play food and crockery. Teacher Sally, observing and writing a report on Myron's activity, said, "Good, you're a good cook, Myron."

> Aaron completed a finger painting. Teacher Lesley: "Aaron, that's real pretty; that's a real good tree. Put it in your bag to take home in the hallway."

> "Cyndy, that's good; put your picture in your bag when you're finished."

> Teacher Sally observed Myron's difficulty in fitting a series of interlocking boxes into each other. She asked, "What's wrong?" and proceeded to assist him until he mastered the spatial dimension and then praised him for his success. "Good, Myron, real good."

Teacher Sally to aimless children in the north classroom:
"Does anyone need a toy? Adam, come over here. I have
something good for you to do."

Casey sat in the reading corner in one of the classrooms
holding an unopened book. Teacher Sally went up to him,
sat down, opened the book and read the story to him. When
she had completed the story, she said, "Now, you read the
book to yourself, O.K.? and look at the pictures." Casey
continued to sit and only looked at the open page. Teacher
Sally: "Let's go in the art room and see what's there for you,
O.K.?" and she led Casey next door.

The children were encouraged to be busy and productive,
all their products being duly deposited in their bags lining the
corridor. At the end of the morning, the mothers would take
the children's products out of the bags and take them home.
Departure time was frequently filled with parental praise and
reinforcement: "Oh, how pretty," "Did you make that?"
"That's real good," "Is that for Mommy?"
The practice of "making things to take home to show the
parents" was an important motivation factor in activity and
clearly exemplified successful task-engagement to both
teachers and parents. It appeared that many of the activities
were geared toward that goal.

Teacher Judy to student volunteer: "Are their paintings dry
yet? No? Oh, well, then they can't put them in their bags
yet."

The children were very enthusiastic about their bags, and
"going home time" assumed a special significance. There
were attendant rituals of behavior:

Teacher Sally: "O.K., everyone, go very quietly and get
your coats and take your bag downstairs with you. If you're
ready, you can sit against the wall right there. Jeremy is the
first one ready today. When children are ready, they should
be sitting down; then I'll know who's ready." As parents
arrived, children delved into their bags, handing the
collection of things to their mothers, and returned the bag to
the teacher. The air was filled with loud exclamations of
excitement. The noise level increased and children were
disorderly as they prepared to leave.

This was the only time period when I observed "disorderly" behavior which was sanctioned by the staff. Teachers smiled, chatted, and laughed with the parents and children at "going-home time," and the children would engage in frequent rough play and loud laughter without reprimand, reflecting the "out-of-school" or "playground" behavior commonly observed in public schooling. The children already discriminated between "rough play" and "school behavior" and internalized this division by the appropriate behaviors. The old maxim "There's a time and place for everything" was evidently effectively learned by these young preschoolers in relation to their "schooling" experience. It appeared that the majority of children were successful in this setting, and willingly followed the norms of the school, where staff authority was mediated through a tight system of controls which nevertheless emanated from a base of positive regard and affection for the children.

A System of Benevolent Controls

The teachers tell you what to do all the time—you can't tell them what you want to do ... It's a yukkie poo-poo school.[3]

The staff rarely behaved punitively to the children. I did not observe a child being punished during the year of observation visits. Teachers relied on the use of rules, reasoned explanation, orders couched in the form of requests, and occasional threats:

Teacher Sally to children not participating in clean-up time: "Children who don't clean up, don't get snacks and that's a rule we've always had." The children immediately responded.

On many occasions, teachers would pose a rational choice to the children, ostensibly allowing them to decide between alternatives.

At 9:15, Teacher Sally said, "Would anyone like to come upstairs and play?" Only a few children went. At 9:19, Teacher Judy shepherded the rest upstairs.

At 9:15 on another morning, Student Teacher Anne called out, "Does anyone want to go and play upstairs?" I stood up, realizing that within five minutes no one would be left in the basement and wondered if the children realized that too.

When the children arrived in the morning, teachers would say, "Would you like to hang your coat up?" or "Would you like to take off your boots?" I did not observe any children replying, "No."

During winter time, children were permitted to play down-stairs in lieu of outside time. Teacher Lesley came down-stairs and asked, "Who wants to go and play a game up-stairs?" Two children shook their heads and refused. Teacher Lesley: "But it really is a fun game—then you can come back." The children acquiesced.

In reality, the children had no freedom. They had the free-dom to take the right option but not the wrong one. Behind the illusion of free choice lay an imperative couched within a framework of *forced choice*—a latent, rather than manifest, characteristic of the teachers' power. The staff never displayed blatant authoritarianism, although an analysis of their inter-actions indicated a clear control paradigm.

Frequently, a conflict would arise between the devel-opmental needs of the *child-at-play* and the schedule and cognitive needs of the *teachers-at-work*.

After a clean-up time, Teacher Sally explained the game, "Doggie, Doggie, Where's Your Bone?" Each child's im-mediate reaction was to look behind for the bone. Teacher Sally: "No, no, you can't look." Bradley, the child in the center, was then told to close his eyes and drop the bone behind someone. Bradley began to crawl around like a dog. Teacher Sally: "Can you *walk* around the circle *normally?*" When the children continued playing the game "wrongly," Teacher Sally, after reprimanding, said, "We have no more time to play. We have to go upstairs and have snacks." (There was still five minutes to go until snack time.)

The teacher clearly was asking the children to display blind obedience to the rules of the game, to view them as absolute. However, if we invoke Piaget at this point,[4] we see a "preoperational" child believing in the imaginary bone and displaying a typical form of egocentrism, in which his conception of the bone is tied to his own actions. Bradley was called a dog—so *he acted like a doggie.* He could not conceive of the dog before acting like the dog (action precedes operational thought) and to ask him to walk "normally" was to destroy the game of "Doggie, Doggie, Where's Your Bone?" It was apparent that the children had ingeniously restructured the game according to their conception of the world and this fell into stark conflict with Teacher Sally's ideal of the correct rules of the game.

> During "free play," Jerry tried to climb "into" a fire game taking place within the block area. Two other children shouted, "But you can't go in." Teacher Lesley, who was watching, said, "Here's another firehat so he can play in the fire too." The two boys who were holding brooms shouted, "No, we can't play in it. It might burn us. We have to squirt it." Teacher Lesley: "I don't want you to climb with brooms; you might fall and it could hurt you." Two boys: "But we need to squirt the fire." Teacher Lesley, "You can only sweep the floor."

Teacher Lesley failed to understand the fantasy play of the two boys, who were living the play world of the fireman. When Jerry tried to play, he threatened to break the rules of the game by *walking into the fire.* The children clearly knew that we don't walk into fire: fire is dangerous and hence Jerry could not walk *into fire.* Teacher Lesley construed the children's statement as an exclusion; she was not willing to flow with the children's fantasy and did not understand that the brooms represented firehoses, not things to climb with. Her statement at the end bore no relation to the make-believe world of fires, which to the two participants seemed an intense experience. To be told to sweep the floor with a broom that had been magically converted to a firehose was a patent violation of the children's experience!

The teachers consciously assumed roles that were distinct and apart from the world of the child; they were never participants, and the lines between staff and children were clearly accentuated.

During story time, Bradley asked Teacher Judy, "Who made that train?" and pointed to a new construction on the wall. Teacher Lesley replied, "*We* made it—the teachers made it."

The teachers conceived of themselves as a separate class— power was delegated to them by the parents and the system of controls was mediated through benevolent authoritarianism. When that failed, peer pressure could frequently be utilized as an incentive to obedience.

During story time, children were told by Teacher Lesley to sit down and listen to a story about bears. Mitch continued to talk and make a noise. Teacher Lesley reprimanded him, "No, Mitch, no." Mitch responded by pointing at Teacher Lesley. Teacher Lesley: "You be quiet, Mitch." Mitch: "No, *you* be quiet"; and he jumped around disrupting the story. Teacher Lesley: "Mitch, don't, honey." Mitch, "Ssshhh," and engaged in a scuffle with two other children. Teacher Lesley ignored him and began the story. Mitch lay down and listened. After the story, Teacher Lesley asked the children questions about the story that pertained to character identification and sequence. She praised the right answers: "Good, Bobby, good." Earl then lay on Jonni's legs. Jonni whined and Teacher Lesley gently re- monstrated, "Get off, honey, get off." When Earl did not acquiesce, other children began to shout, "Get off," "Quit that," "Get off," simultaneously. Teacher Lesley got up and lifted him off Jonni's legs.

Conflict

Another striking characteristic of this school was an emphasis on teaching children to play together and share. Social inter- action and social skills were valued as highly as their cognitive counterparts.

There was a consistent concern manifested by the staff for *excluded* children, and potential conflicts were handled by swift intervention prior to escalation.

Teacher Sally was building with Jerry in one of the class- rooms. Mitch walked up. "I want to play too." Teacher

Sally: "Jerry, if Mitch wants to play with you, share those with him." Jerry complied, and soon another child joined the twosome and all three played together.

Reasoned explanation was a tactic frequently employed by both Teacher Lesley and Teacher Sally when they intervened. They actively encouraged children to verbalize anger, and there was a rigid "no hurting" rule which included no hitting, pushing, pulling, name calling, pinching, etc. The incidents of conflict invariably appeared in the free play time.

During free play time there was an unusually high noise level today. Annie leveled a series of insults at her friend Mary and then pinched her. Teacher Sally: "No, don't pinch. It feels really bad to be pinched." Annie listened and walked off.

Seth tried to grab a toy telephone away from a new little girl. Teacher Sally, who stood up, saw me watching, sat down again and waited. When Seth tried a second time, Teacher Sally told him to stop and said, "Here's another phone. When she's playing with a toy, don't take it." A few minutes later the new little girl wandered off. Teacher Sally to Seth: "Is anyone playing with that toy now? No? O.K., then you can play with it."

Teacher Anne to Mitch, who tried to climb into a toy house under protest from another child: "I don't think Timmy wants you in there now. You have to wait your turn."

Toward the end of free play time, one child started shouting. Both Teacher Sally and a new volunteer *rushed* over (I thought the rushing disproportionate to the shouting). Aaron and Mitch were both tugging at opposite ends of the plank. Aaron was crying (lightly) because Mitch had hit him. When Teacher Sally arrived, Mitch hit her. Teacher Sally (very calmly, but sternly): "Mitch, *you can get mad at me, but you can't hit me.*" The fight ceased and the children went on playing.

While the teachers believed in acknowledging the angry feelings of the children, they actively fostered self-control and the repression of physical anger and placed a high premium on post-hoc verbalization. While these children were certainly verbal, their first spontaneous reaction often appeared to be couched in a *physical*, rather than *verbal*, mode of expression.

Teacher Sally told me that they encourage children to say, "Stop hitting me. I don't like people hitting me," and that one of their goals was to encourage the children to resolve conflict on their own—that there should not be immediate intervention unless a dangerous situation was seen to develop. While this permissive attitude was expressed verbally, I observed only one instance of hesitation on the part of any staff member, and that occurred when she was aware of my presence. The norm appeared to be that of a denial of conflict in favor of a strong socialization toward order, structure, and harmony.

On a number of occasions minor scuffles would occur where one child would lightly hit another without any apparent reaction. Whenever this was observed, a staff member would immediately intervene and stop it. Play that was construed as potentially disruptive was also curbed:

> Jerry rolled a wheel in the direction of a small group, shouting, "Tiger's coming." Teacher Lesley: "I don't like that; that's not a good idea; O.K.?"

> Myron walked around, sucking his fingers. He climbed up to the top of the slide and stood there. Three children stood behind him. Teacher Sally: "Myron, are you coming down the slide?" Myron: "No." Teacher Sally: "I think you ought to." Myron: "Why?" Teacher Sally: "It's not a good idea [to stand there]." Myron slid down.

> Annie and Aaron were playing "tennis" downstairs. Each time Aaron missed, he said, "Do-do ball." Teacher Sally: "Aaron, if you don't hit the ball, does that make the ball a do-do? Call it 'you tennis ball,' O.K.? Not do-do." Annie: "I said *no-do* ball." Teacher Sally: "I heard you, Annie." Annie: "You do-do ball, do-do ball, do-do ball." Teacher Sally: "Do you think *you* like being called do-do?" (Turns to look at me and shrugs with raised eyebrows.)

While staff were usually present to intervene in any potentially disruptive incidents, there were a number of occasions when I, the only adult present, witnessed peer intervention unmediated by teachers.

> Sandra and Mary were fighting over a colored pitcher. Sandra said, after a few minutes of unsuccessful tugging, "Put it in the middle and then we can both use it."

At the water table, Aaron hit Mitch. Two other children standing nearby shouted, "Hey, cut it out. Quit that." Aaron replied, "Ssshhh," and stopped.

Sandra tried to join Debra in clay-making upstairs, and Debra shouted, "Dummy," and chased her away.

Aaron grabbed the wooden iron from Myron in the fantasy play area. Myron shouted, "No, I do it." He wrested the iron from Aaron and prepared to hit him on the head with it. As Aaron ducked, I put up my hand to block the blow. Myron ran away and hid the iron.

During my visits to this school, I had been surprised by the *low* incidence of aggression and conflict that I found. I was simultaneously observing at other centers and had encountered a different set of behaviors there. I realized after witnessing a series of the above representative incidents that what I had initially construed as a high level of social cooperation was instead the result of effective containment; for within this preschool structure, conflict was perceived as dysfunctional, as detrimental to the order and stability of the environment. Children were socialized to "get along with other kids" and "to follow directions." Inter-child and staff-child conflict was thus considered systemically disruptive.

When we examine the structural properties of this nursery school, we notice that its features approximate a microsocial equilibrium model organized along lines of certainty, security, and predictability and closed to fundamental alternations of the planned time curriculum. We find limited freedom within a framework of nonfreedom.

We note a strategy of conflict-management and containment on the part of the staff which, in turn, relates to a pervasive "order" model in early childhood training programs (see chapter 9 for a full discussion of this issue).

Furthermore, as the expression of aggression was viewed as negative and disruptive to the status quo, the need for self-assertion was rarely recognized. In all but one cited observation, the staff intervened *before* the development of manifested aggression; Myron's iron-blow attack occurred when controls were absent, i.e., when no teachers were present.

It was evident that the constant attentiveness on the part of the staff fostered an outwardly conflict-free environment.

Their organized and efficient program and their dedication to the "order" component of life was girded by the active socialization of the children into institutionalized time. When the children were "directed-in-time," the landscape was ordered and "in balance" and warmth and a positive social experience were seen to emerge. This social structure thus generated a system of controls which aimed toward the *minimization of temporal, spatial, and interpersonal disruption.*

5
Busy Bee
Montessori Center

The Busy Bee Montessori Center is a one-story brick building in a suburban area of a Midwestern city. The center has a large outside play area with climbing equipment, and the program offerings include two morning classes for toddlers, a preschool and a kindergarten that run until 3:30 each day. The center is a private, nonprofit, accredited Montessori institution with a licensed preschool staff who have additional Montessori qualifications as well as a number of assistant teachers who are not licensed but have undergone Montessori training. The majority of the children are drawn from white middle-income families although a limited number of financial scholarships are available for low-income families.

While I spent two years as an observer at this center moving between the toddler classes, the preschool, and kindergarten, it was the former group that most attracted my interest;[1] for in this environment it was possible to witness firsthand the power of the Montessori socialization experience for babies between one-and-a-half and two-and-a-half years of age, for whom this was a first institutionalization experience. Hence, most of the observations that follow are extracted from the toddler program.

The toddler classroom comprised one large rectangular room with a climbing apparatus and foot bar placed in the entrance hall. This was the only piece of large motor equipment. Throughout the room there were small tables with one chair each, and there were also three tables with two chairs each. Montessori mats were provided for those children who wished to work on the floor. Specially designed Montessori cognitive materials were placed around the perimeter of the room on shelves. Each set of materials occupied a designated place, to which it had to be returned after use.

During the first hour, the toddlers were free to move about the room and to choose to "work" with any of the available materials. The last half hour was devoted to "circle" time, when singing, exercises and group cognitive activities took place. In mild weather, ten to fifteen minutes would be spent outside prior to departure.

The Work Ethic

Among the revelations the child has brought us,
there is one of fundamental importance, the
phenomenon of normalization through work ... It is
certain that the child's aptitude for work represents
a vital instinct; for without work, his personality
cannot organize itself and deviates from the normal
lines of its construction. Man builds himself
through working.[2]

Upon entry into the Montessori classroom, I was struck by the remarkable orderliness of the environment, the tidiness of the classroom, and the fact that there was virtual silence in a room filled with twelve toddlers and two teachers. The ordered state of the room was constant, i.e., there was no change in appearance between entry and exit time. As the infants entered the room, they were greeted by teachers, taught how to take off their jackets and hang them up on a coat hanger, and then encouraged to find "work" to do.

There were a number of rules pertaining to work which the teachers spent a great deal of time teaching to the children:

a. All work was to be fetched from the shelves, laid on a table or floor mat, and replaced in the exact spot after completion.

b. When children had been working at tables, chairs had to be pushed in before work was returned to the shelves.

c. No child could interfere with another child's work.

d. No running or rough play or shouting was permitted in the classroom.

During the fall, the entry point of most of the toddlers, almost all of my observations centered around work-related instructions and interactions.

Work and Possession

Celia entered the class a few weeks after its inception. She investigated the environment and the materials, and obediently put work back when told to do so by the teachers. She saw a puzzle of Pete's lying on the table and went to put that away, too. Teacher Martha: "Celia, that is Pete's work." Pete was then instructed to retrieve the work, place it back on the table and then return it to its original place on the shelf. At this point, Celia wandered off to another shelf and picked up play animals. Teacher Martha *ran* over. "Celia, you left your work out. Put that back and put this work away first—no, push your chair in first and then put it away."

Later Jomo walked up to Celia's table. Teacher Martha: "Jomo, this is Celia's work." Celia did not seem to mind Jomo's presence as she said, "Help me there." Jomo put out his hand but Teacher Martha intervened. "Jomo, this is Celia's work. Can you find something else to do?" Jomo wandered off to Bruce's table and touched his work. Teacher Jackie: "This is Bruce's work." At that point, Jomo dropped the storybook he was carrying, and was told to put his own work back.

Jeremy and Leroi stood up from a double table. Sharon and Paul took their seats and continued a weight activity. Teacher Jackie: "This is Jeremy's work. This is Leroi's work." She called the latter two back. "Put it back on the shelf, please." Jeremy: "I don't want it." Teacher Martha: "Well, I'll help you with it and then Sharon and Paul can take it to the shelf again." She explains to Paul, "Paul, this is Jeremy's work. He needs to put it away before you can take it."

Alan prepared to thread large beads at another table after leaving a bowl of small beads (which he could not thread) on a previous table. Teacher Jackie: "I'm *glad* you want to do that but you're going to have to come down and put away all those beads in this bowl first." Alan squealed a protest and did not do as he was told. Teacher Jackie picked him up, laid him flat on his stomach and forced him through physical pressure to pick them up while she remained bending over him.

Janey took Sandi's hanger and tried to hang it up for her. Teacher Jackie: "Janey, that is Sandi's hanger. Sandi, can you hang up your *own* hanger, please?"

Montessori believed that satisfying engagement and absorption in work led to the formulation of a system of inner controls, a sense of personal fulfillment which facilitated the development of an *inner* strength and self-discipline on the part of the child.[3] Due to an earlier family socialization process where the *inner* discipline had not been sufficiently stressed, it was necessary to establish an external locus of control in the classroom whereby the children would "internalize the external" and thus be given the correct momentum for intrinsic discipline and motivation, which Montessori assumed was fundamental to child nature. As "work" was considered the *mode* basic to the development of the self, the practical translation of this work ethic assumed a series of training periods in the classroom.

During the first four months in the Montessori classroom, I observed that children were taught to discriminate "my work" from the "other's work," i.e., work isolation. This tended to encourage insular rather than interactive behavior among the children. In this context, Janey transgressed the norm by helping Sandi to hang up her coat. Possession of work followed initial isolation, and this, in turn, led to work ownership; and for the duration of activity engagement or absorption, work was sacred property and no violations were tolerated.

The vocabulary employed by the teachers personified the work and tended to depersonalize the children.

Kyle entered the classroom and walked up to Sven, smiled, and tried to play with him. Teacher Jackie: "Kyle, please don't bother Sven's work."

Jomo ran up to the table that Kyle was working at and pushed it over, spilling the work. Kyle, who had been crying sporadically the whole morning, began to scream. Teacher Jackie took Jomo, sat him down against the wall and said, "You don't push *other people's work* down." Teacher Jackie then helped to pick up Kyle's work but did not comfort him. He continued to cry sporadically until the class ended.

The initial Montessori socialization period—the fall semester—concentrated almost exclusively on commands, instruction, and prohibitions related to work. (During one morning, I counted thirty-eight commands of "Put your work away" in one and a half hours.) The subsequent winter semester was devoted to the "normalization through work" period that Montessori envisioned. The following section considers the implications and related problems ensuing from the work ethic.

Egocentrism and Work Possession

The goals of the "normalization through work" socialization process were described to me by the head teacher of the toddler division:

"When the child enters the Montessori classroom, he is scattered, like hell on wheels. When he comes in he has a short attention span—we make an attempt to educate the child for life—so that he is self-directive, makes decisions for himself and learns how to get along with others." After the child has been in a Montessori classroom, "He has inner control." When I inquired as to the initial emphasis on extreme individuality and work possession, the staff informed me that that was a necessary prerequisite to the above-stated goal.

As we have seen, children were taught to discriminate "my" work from "other's" work and to make the distinction between *possessed-work-while-I-am-engaged-in-it* and *everyone's-work* (open possession / free work) when not in use. Occasionally, however, the teachers would make mistakes:

Jomo took Alan's beads. Alan: "No." Teacher Martha took the beads from Alan and gave them to Jomo. Teacher Jackie came up. "Jomo, this is Alan's work." Teacher Martha to Teacher Jackie: "Oh, I'm sorry, I thought it was Jomo's work." Teacher Jackie: "No, this is Alan's work"; and she sent Jomo off.

Given the Piagetian insights pertaining to the egocentrism of the preoperational stage of development and the fact that this is the period in which the child begins to decenter and to move from extreme egocentrism to a more mature accommodation of the external world,[4] it appeared that the staff were unconsciously fostering regressive egocentrism by insisting on the insularity, possession and ownership of work. The children were *not* able to make the complex discrimination of possession and engagement that the staff had conceptualized; hence, they manifested *increasing*, not *decreasing* individuality and possessiveness, as the months progressed. While initially there had been an admixture of possession and sociable sharing, after a semester of socialization, the children were clearly insistent about their *work* ownership. Once the association between "my work," "my table," "don't bother me," was made, it was developmentally difficult for the children to conceptualize the transition from work respect to social cooperation based on mutual respect, which ostensibly was the ultimate goal of the teachers. We should remember too, that the children in this Montessori class from whom a sophisticated taxonomy of ownership and sharing was expected were *barely two years old.*

In the following citations, we observe the children after four months of Montessori training:

Jomo went up to Celia and touched her work. She shouted, "That's mine. That's mine." Jomo laughed and ran off.

Lesley was absorbed in cutting small pieces of paper. As any child approached her, she squealed and repeated, "This my work. This my chair. This my table."

Alan carried blocks over to Kyle, with whom he had previously been playing on the climbing bar (one of the few collective activities). He put the blocks onto the table Kyle was sitting at. Kyle: "Take that off my table. This my table." Alan threw the blocks on the floor. Kyle shouted, "Stop it," and picked the blocks up and tried to put them on Alan's table.

Jimmy tried to take Kyle's mat to use as Kyle was in the process of putting it away. Kyle grabbed it back. "No, this my work. I do it myself." He rolled up the mat and put it away himself. Jimmy waited and then unrolled it to use.

Paul, the youngest child at eighteen months, walked to Lesley's table and touched her on the shoulder, smiling, seem-

ingly wanting to play. Lesley yelled, "Don't touch me."
Teacher Jackie stood and watched as Paul continued to
touch Lesley and she continued to yell, "Don't touch me,"
while enfolding her work with her arms. Teacher Jackie then
said, "Can you say, 'Please go away,' to Paul?" Lesley hit and
pushed him and Paul said, "No, no push." Teacher Jackie
did *not* intervene and Paul toddled off, whimpering.

A climate of hostility and unfriendliness emerged among
these children, which appeared to be related to the way in
which they restructured the rules of their "work" environment.
Sociability, which often involved touching, was construed as
work interference or potential work violation. The friendly
child in this school structure began to be regarded as the interloper, the enemy, the threat to work sovereignty. We see reflected here a pattern of discontinuity, a paradox between the
latent and manifest socialization goals and, perhaps, a paradigm
in microcosm of the emergence and development of the
capitalist ethic. This was exemplified by the move from work
insularity to work possession to work ownership, with the con-
comitant attitudes of hostile regard and alienation from one's
neighbor.

Another interesting feature of this environment related to the
perception of conflict, which was inextricably bound to the
"work" ideal situated within the social landscape of the Montessori classroom.

Work and Conflict

Conflict was regarded as "natural," owing to the ego-centered
personality of the child (this was explained to me by head
teacher Jackie), but was believed to stem from lack of work
involvement. It was assumed that engaged and absorbed children would have no need for conflict; thus the assumptions
about the origins of conflict were rooted in an object-centered,
not a person-centered, view of social relationships. Most of the
observed conflicts were seen to center on work.

Raina went up to Kyle and looked over his shoulder and tried
to take a block. Teacher Jackie: "Don't bother Kyle's work,
Raina." Kyle then hit Raina on the head with a block.
Teacher Jackie to Kyle: "Say, 'Raina, please don't bother my

work.'" Raina continued to annoy Kyle. Teacher Jackie: "Raina, you're making Kyle very angry." At that point, Jason walked up and looked at Kyle's work. Kyle picked up his chair and hit Jason with it. Jason fell down crying. Teacher Jackie picked up Jason asking him *if he fell*. She then explained to him that he was "bothering Kyle's work." At no point did the teacher reprimand Kyle for hitting Raina or Jason.

Raina upset Kyle's work and overturned the table. He hit her on the head. Raina did not react but continued to "bother" Kyle. Kyle began to scream. Teacher Martha: "Raina, Kyle doesn't like to have his work bothered." She took Raina to another table and told Kyle to tell Raina, "Don't bother my work."

Molly overturned Marissa's bowl of sticks. Teacher Marian ran over to Molly, who had dashed off, and said, "No, you may not spill the work. No, you may not spill the work," and brought Molly back to pick it up as Marissa dissolved into tears. "This is Marissa's work. Marissa, you need to tell Molly, 'No, this is my work.'"

A peculiar phenomenon emerged here. While the staff unequivocally stressed a prohibition of all forms of physical aggression ("No child may hurt another") and an approach of "getting the child to verbalize his anger," there was an inherent paradox within this policy which related to the violation of work rules. Conflict appeared to be sanctioned when a child's right to pursue individual work satisfaction was transgressed. In those instances the conflict was explained in work-related terms. In one and a half years of observation, I only observed five exceptions to this pattern, of which the following is representative:

Kyle hit Raina for trying to take his work. Raina cried. Teacher Marian (holding Raina): "Kyle doesn't like you to bother his work. That's why he hit you." She then said to Kyle, "Kyle, don't hit, *tell* Raina not to bother your work."

In these instances, the "aggressor" was told not to hit but rather to verbalize; no attention was given to the feelings of the children or to the source or cause of aggression, as it was assumed to stem from lack of work involvement. The teachers frequently appeared to deny the angry intentions of the children when directed at themselves or at other children. They also masked the outward manifestations of their own anger or irritation with the children through the medium of soft-spoken tones and an intensely quiet voice to indicate disapproval. I only witnessed one incident where Teacher Jackie actually shouted at a child. Most interactions were typically of the following order:

> Noah pushed Kennie off his chair, and Kennie cried. Teacher Jackie: "I think Noah wanted to *help* you onto the chair." (My perception was that Noah intended to push Kennie off the chair.)

> Raina had been persistently pursued for the first half hour of the morning by Teacher Martha and told to "Put your work away." Raina evaded Teacher Martha and ran up to the shelf, took a bowl of beads, turned it over and threw all the beads out, laughed and looked at Teacher Martha. Teacher Martha (very quietly and calmly): "Oh, oh, Raina had an *accident*. Please pick them up." (My perception was that Raina had deliberately overturned the beads.)

The persistent denial of angry intentions and, in certain instances, of expressions of rebellion created an atmosphere of deception. The teachers, in many cases, were clearly aware of the children's intentions, yet chose to mask this through pretense. This approach fostered an ultimate denial of interpersonal responsibility on the part of both the staff and their young charges. The intentionality of the child, when it was directed against the structural order, was systematically negated. This issue leads to a consideration of the handling of rebels/deviants within this structure.

Work and Social Deviance

This section of observations will focus on three "rebels": Molly (two years), Jomo (twenty-two months), and Raina (two years, three months). Molly attended the early morning class; Jomo and Raina, the late morning class. The following incidents have been selected because they reveal the real in-

fluence that these three children exerted when they entered in
the fall, the manner in which they resisted Montessori socialization, and the way this resistance was perceived and handled
by the staff and their parents.

Molly

Two-year-old Molly was an active, independent little girl who
constantly moved about the classroom. She did not appear to
derive satisfaction from sedentary "work" and defied the
teachers when told to "sit down" or "do work." She was frequently a "disruptive" influence during "circle" time when
the children would participate in a half-hour period of singing,
"reading readiness," and other group exercises. Staff members
regarded Molly as a "problem."

> During circle time, Molly would not sit still. She jumped
> up and down and was taken onto Teacher Jackie's lap
> and held in a vicelike grip. She cried, kicked, and squealed,
> and the "Hunter Song" was interrupted to the annoy-
> ance of the teachers. Teacher Jackie then let her go,
> and she ran to take a book from the chair. Teacher Jackie
> removed the book and pulled her back on her lap, and the
> protest was repeated. Teacher Jackie then asked Teacher
> Marian to call the name cards. Molly's name was called last.

> At another circle activity, Molly again refused to sit still.
> Teacher Jackie remarked to Teacher Marian: "Molly is
> going to pesterize everyone around her till I can't stand it."
> The children's name cards were called—PPPaul, BBBrian,
> etc. When Molly's was called, she did not respond. Teacher
> Jackie, holding her on her lap, tapped her. She would not
> answer. She was then removed from the circle and made to
> sit on the outside. At this point, she answered, putting up
> two hands instead of one.

Molly rarely bothered other children during circle time. She
only became "disruptive" and "bothersome" when forced to
sit in the circle, or when told to do something by the teachers.
When left alone, however, she frequently became absorbed in
activities which were not considered conducive to classroom
harmony.

> Molly, after resisting circle time for well over a week, was
> "left alone" by the teachers as a new tactic. Unseen by the

staff, she took off her shoes and socks and spent fifteen minutes absorbed in drawing pictures on her fingers and toes. She utilized different colors of chalk, tried to erase the chalk with an eraser, and did not utter a word. When Teacher Jackie turned around and noticed what Molly was doing, she grabbed the chalk from her saying, "You don't draw on feet. Chalk is for the chalk board. You don't take your shoes and socks off in class." When Molly's chalk was removed, she screamed and kicked and threw herself on the floor.

Molly clearly did not like her will thwarted. She initiated her own activities, attributing different functions to the classroom materials. From my vantage point as an observer, I had been fascinated by the intense concentration meted out to her body drawing and the way in which she utilized the eraser. In so doing, she manifested a rather typical age-pattern of exploratory behavior, where things (chalk and erasers) have many unlimited possibilities to be experimented with and acted upon in a world of "beckoning objects." Here the function of the eraser was generalized from blackboard to feet, in much the same way that another toddler will use a scrubbing brush to brush hair! Molly's actions were rather "normal" and relatively harmless, yet in a "school" setting such as this the typical was transformed to the deviant, eliciting reprimand and punishment by her teachers.

Molly's pattern of screaming became more and more common as the months ensued, and frequently the teachers would threaten her, the threats always couched in ambiguous language and quiet tones.

As Molly picked up some work to do, Teacher Marian announced, "Put-away-work time." Molly did not listen and pulled out a chair. Teacher Marian: "No, it's time to put away work. Molly, we're going to sit down now." Molly shouted, "No," and lay on the table screaming. Teacher Jackie (very quietly): "Do you want to sit down by yourself or do you want me to *help* you?" Molly: "No." (Kicks.) Teacher Jackie picked her up, held her by the scruff of her sweater like a cat, and deposited her on Teacher Marian's lap. Molly kicked, screamed, and struggled. Other children began to move out of the newly formed circle and were called back. The circle was rearranged, with restless children seated near the teachers. Hardly any child sang as the teachers went through the song repertoire amid Molly's screaming. After ten minutes she was let loose. She went to sit by herself at the original table she had chosen and sat quietly looking at a book.

Warren tried to grab a book from Molly as circle time began. Molly screamed. Teacher Marian intervened and separated them. "Warren, leave Molly. Molly, sit up." Brian then took the book from Molly. She screamed again. Teacher Jackie grabbed her, gave her the book and told her to put it away. Molly refused. "Will you or must I put it back for you?" Teacher Jackie then pulled her to the circle while she screamed. Teacher Jackie shook her until she dropped the book and put her on her lap.

After a few months of Montessori experience, Molly not only screamed when teachers interfered with her, but generalized this to her peers. This reaction developed over time as a feature of the classroom environment, for Molly had not manifested such behavior upon entry. She also appeared to dislike both teachers' laps, which represented to my mind a symbol of containment rather than comfort. Molly was never taken on a lap for a cuddle or warm interaction but as a form of control over impulses which clashed with the structural norms. I often wondered how she associated laps-in-general, outside of the Montessori environment—were they, too, symbols of struggle rather than comfort?

During one visit, while I was sitting in the classroom waiting for the children to be picked up, the following conversation took place between Molly's mother and Teacher Jackie:

Teacher Jackie: "She's very busy when she's here, but seems angry, still won't sit down and seems to have a chip on her shoulder." Mother: "We've really been trying," and then explained that her older brother bullies her. "Maybe she learns this through having it done to her; at home she is self-directive and independent. We have our problems with her. She wants to dress herself. She's further advanced than the others—has the personality of her grandmother." Teacher Jackie: "She seems to have a chip on her shoulder."

Upon later enquiry, I learned that Molly's mother had been approached previously about Molly's problems and this was a follow-up conversation. Her mother spoke defensively; while acknowledging her daughter's sense of self-assertion, she conceded that it was problematical, and moved from sibling to hereditary rationalizations to explain the "problem" behavior. Molly continued to pose problems within that class for the duration of two semesters and then left.

Jomo

Twenty-two-month-old Jomo was a friendly, boisterous, black little boy whose weapon of rebellion was *laughter*. In all the months that I observed this class, I never heard Jomo cry or scream. When thwarted or reprimanded, he would dissolve into chortles or gurgles of laughter, which irritated the staff. He initiated many disruptions in the class, would not sit and "work," and constantly sought out other children to "play." Upon entering the classroom in the morning, Jomo always greeted other children, but no one answered.

> Jomo entered laughing, ran into the room and shouted, "Hi." No one answered. He repeated himself, shouting louder, "I say, hi." No one answered. He continued to greet other children as they entered without reply.

After Jomo entered the classroom, one of the two teachers would take responsibility for "chasing after" him and rechanneling his "disruptive energies."

> Jomo overturned the trash can, and pulled out all the soiled kleenex. He laughed uproariously and Kyle and Sandi ran to join him. Teacher Jackie hurried over. "Did you have an *accident*, Jomo?" (I thought it was deliberate.) She sent him off to take some work. He scampered away, laughing, and ran around the table. She went up to him, put her hands *solemnly* on his head and said very quietly, "Jomo, settle down." He again ran away, took the kleenex box, and began pulling out one tissue after another, chuckling. Teacher Jackie: "No, Jomo, this is for blowing our noses."

I recorded the following note to myself after three visits to the school.

> Jomo is an amazingly active and very affectionate child. He always comes up to greet me unlike the other children. I find his mischievousness endearing and amusing. So much of his naughtiness appears typical of a lively twenty-two-

month-old who would rather run and play than be confined to work!

One of the "problems" with Jomo was that he would not "work," and he introduced continual constellations of disorder in the classroom with children who would follow him.

Jomo ran to the door, which was always kept closed, and opened it. Two children followed him. He banged the door loudly and laughed. Both Anthony and Pete followed suit, and within seconds the three had created a commotion. Teacher Jackie told them to come in and close the door. Jomo banged it shut and laughed. Teacher Jackie whispered, "Let's close the door quietly, like this." Anthony then banged it shut and all three shouted with laughter. Teacher Jackie: "Will you please go find some work to do?"

Kyle and Jomo were taken to the bathroom together and came back running through the door. Jomo pushed Kyle and Kyle accidentally overturned Lesley's beads on the mat. Lesley: "Oh, no." Teacher Martha called Jomo to pick them up. Teacher Jackie then told them to reenter, commenting very quietly, "That was terrible." Lesley echoed, "That was terrible." Lesley went on working and singing as she worked alone. Kyle and Jomo went up and said, "Hi." Lesley: "No, I working here." Teacher Jackie said, "Lesley, say, 'Please go away.'"

A new little girl, Terri, entered the class halfway through the semester. As she entered no one but Jomo evinced any interest in her or looked up from work. Jomo ran up, saying, "Hi." She followed him around the room while Teacher Martha looked on, seemingly uncomfortable. A little later, she both scratched and then hugged him. Jomo laughed and jumped around. At this point, Teacher Martha separated them and told Jomo to "Go find some work to do," while she took charge of the new little girl.

The response of the other children to the newcomer was interesting. They were too absorbed in their *work* as individuals to notice her, and neither of the teachers introduced or made a fuss of the child. Jomo, in fact, was the only sociable person in the environment, greeting Terri and playing with her. She responded to him and was separated from his influence soon after entry. While it was clear to me that Jomo was viewed as disruptive by the teachers, it seemed that many of the children, over time, began to view him in this fashion too.

Jomo entered with his usual "Hi," followed by a smile. He went up to Kyle and touched him with a friendly pat and smiled. Kyle hit him saying, "I don't like that boy." Jomo ran off and went up to Celia and did the same. She squealed and covered her work. Teacher Jackie: "Jomo, go find some work to do." She tells Teacher Marian, "Get him work to do and spend time with him—I'll take care of the rest of the class." Teacher Marian took him by the hand, led him away from the others, and muttered, "Has he been measured yet?" A little while later, Jomo ran up to Celia and hugged her. She screamed. Teacher Marian to Celia: "Did he try to give you a hug? Jomo, Celia doesn't like that. Let's find some work for you to do."

Jomo's sociability and friendliness were interpreted as work interference by the toddlers themselves. The toddlers had restructured the message of this environment, i.e., the only valid interactions are those that center around work. They, in fact, appeared to be manifesting hostility, a fierce work possessiveness, and a preference for being alone which I found unusual for babies of that age. The rapid socialization of these children in this particular setting was unparalleled in any other age group or school under consideration. I construed this to be a feature of their extremely young age interacting with a rigorous socialization process. How then did Jomo escape this?

As mentioned earlier, he laughed continually. In addition, he rarely seemed to listen to the staff but would run away when spoken to. There were also a small number of children who would sporadically engage in disruption with him, forming a temporary alliance. However, Jomo's main ally in the classroom was Raina—a two-year-old little girl who was both defiant and "aggressive" to other children. Before discussing Raina, however, it might be useful to cite what actions the staff took on "disruptive children" like Jomo.

In a discussion with Teacher Jackie, she told me she is considering recommending psychological evaluation for Jomo. When I enquired why, she replied, "He hasn't gotten himself together; he is very distractible; he runs around all the time; he really likes other children but he has problems with himself; he doesn't stay with any activities."

Jomo, with his transgression of sociability, was thus labeled by Teacher Jackie during another conversation as "hyperactive, although clinically, I suppose, he's not." This same teacher later did recommend psychological evaluation, and he was sent, ironically, to play therapy for treatment!

Raina

Raina entered late and was immediately shepherded in the direction of an activity although she tried to greet other children. She sat down at a table with "work" and soon rose to put it away and went to sit at another table. Teacher Martha: "No, Raina, you have to push your chair back first." Raina did so, saying, "There," loudly. Teacher Martha nodded acknowledgment. Raina took a set of dominoes off the shelf but within minutes was up again, going to fetch a second set. Teacher Martha stopped her and sat her back on her chair. She jumped up and ran to another table. Teacher Martha: "You need to put your work away." Raina did not listen, and Teacher Martha physically dragged her back to her original work, held her arm, thereby forcibly ensuring that she replaced the work and pushed her chair in. When Raina was released from Teacher Martha's hold, she took new work, and Jomo came up and began to play with the work. Both teachers: "This is Raina's work. This is Raina's work." At that moment Raina ran away, grabbed a bowl containing vast numbers of small beads, overturned the bowl, and laughed as hundreds of beads scattered over the floor. Teacher Martha: "Oh, oh, Raina had an accident."

Marty was sitting at a table looking at a book. Raina ran up and pointed to a picture in the book. Marty held the book and said, "No." Raina grabbed the book and ran away. Teacher Jackie gave the book back to Marty and took Raina to another table. "You *may not* take other people's work; you *may* take things from the shelf."

Raina appeared outwardly defiant during her hours in the classroom, and a frequent act of rebellion on her part was to actively destroy the order of the classroom. Throwing or overturning was a common action, which the teachers, in turn,

denied. The negation of Raina's intentionality and the labeling of her defiance as accidental occurred repeatedly.

While Raina was defiant in the classroom, her entry each
morning was a difficult one, and she would cling to her mother
or father, crying in distress. This was not common among her
classmates.

Raina came late today, her mother apologizing to Teacher
Jackie. Raina clung to her mother, crying. The mother extri-
cated herself and, as she was leaving, looked back, and
Teacher Jackie replied, "It's O.K." After her mother left,
Raina lay on the floor sobbing. Jomo went up to her saying,
"Raina, Raina," seemingly concerned. Neither of the
teachers paid any attention to what they termed "Raina's
tantrum." After she stopped crying, Teacher Jackie went up
to her and helped her off with her jacket.

Raina's father brought her into the classroom, still holding
her. Raina was carrying a book, which Teacher Jackie
asked her father to take home. As the father prepared to
leave, Raina began to cry. He cuddled her saying, "Oh, now
don't cry," as Raina clung to him. When he left, Raina lay on
the floor and screamed. Both teachers ignored her until the
crying stopped.

The classroom was a lonely place for Raina. She was
hounded by the teachers and rejected by her peers. Her only
friend appeared to be fellow-deviant Jomo. Once again, the
perception that the teachers held of Raina as a disruptive child
appeared to be related to her nonadjustment to the "work"
ethic.

Jomo and Raina were very excited by the presence of some
newly acquired "squeaky" blocks. They both emptied the
blocks onto the floor and shouted and whooped with
laughter. Other children joined, and the noise level in the
classroom rose. Children were jumping and dancing around
the blocks within minutes. Teacher Martha hurried over
and enforced the "rug rule" (no work on the floor, only on
rugs). Jomo laughed uproariously and the situation approached chaos. Teacher Jackie ran over, asking Jomo, "Is
that your work?" Jomo took a block from Raina, who
laughed. Teacher Jackie: "No, no, this is Raina's work." At
that point, the children were dispersed, leaving Raina and
Jomo at the blocks. Teacher Jackie: "If you don't play

quietly, you'll have to put the blocks away." She then turned to me and said, "This it the first day we've had these blocks." (She neglected to say, "and the last," for, needless to say, the blocks never appeared again in subsequent observation visits.)

After a few months in the classroom, Raina began to "interfere" randomly with other children.

Raina went up to Kyle and scratched his face. Kyle turned to Teacher Jackie. "Raina not my friend." Teacher Jackie: "Have you told Raina not to scratch your face?"

Raina leaned over Bruce's shoulder. He cried and covered his work. Teacher Martha: "No, Raina, you don't bother other people's work." She was taken to sit by herself at a table along the wall. Another child walked past. She hit him hard. He screamed. As he screamed, Jomo came up to Raina and she pulled up a chair for him. Teacher Martha reprimanded Raina and told Jomo to go away from Raina. "You have to learn not to bother other people's work."

Raina approached Lesley and tried to grab her work off the table. Lesley: "No, mine. No, my work." Teacher Jackie: "Say to Raina, 'Please go away.'"

Raina frequently pushed other children and engaged in physical aggression. On one such occasion, after she had repeatedly pushed Bruce (whom she seemed to like), the following occurred:

Bruce pushed Raina and pulled her hair. Raina cried momentarily but stopped. Bruce then touched Raina's work, but she did not react. Teacher Martha: "This is Raina's work." Raina, however, picked up her work and banged it down defiantly on Bruce's table. Teacher Martha: "This is Bruce's table."

Many situations in which Raina was perceived to behave problematically related to the developmental inappropriateness of the work environment and materials provided. Raina was bright and curious and often attempted work which she could not master, unlike the other children, who left complex tasks alone.

Raina left an uncompleted puzzle on the table and put interlocking barrels (her second work) away. Teacher

Martha told her to put her first work away. Raina took the unfinished puzzle and banged it down on a table. Teacher Martha: "That's the wrong place." As she picked up the puzzle, the pieces fell out. Raina picked up the pieces and left them on the table after trying unsuccessfully to complete the puzzle. She then grabbed Celia's work and put it away. Teacher Martha: "Raina, that was Celia's work." Raina then went back to her table, looked at the puzzle, and ran over to the water table. Teacher Martha saw Raina at the water table, dragged her kicking and shouting back to her table, sat down, and helped her to complete the puzzle.

It was evident that Raina could not complete the puzzle and hence could *not* put her work away; for one of the ground rules of Montessori is that all work has to be completed before being returned to the shelf. As Raina could not complete the puzzle, she tried to put Celia's work back and attempted to become involved in another activity. Both acts transgressed a *work rule* which, in these instances, was disconsonant with Raina's level of competence and interest.

During the winter, Raina stopped coming to the school. When I enquired as to the cause of departure, Teacher Jackie made the following comments:

"Raina has left. She has terrible problems. She mauled other children and *seemed to enjoy being naughty*. Her parents don't know what to do with her. She's an adopted child." Jackie told me that she recommended to Raina's parents that she be sent for psychological evaluation. "She has problems—needs some play therapy." Teacher Jackie also informed Raina's parents that she would only be willing to work with the child after they found out "what was *wrong* with her." When I enquired as to the procedures employed by Teacher Jackie in the classroom, she replied, "Putting Raina on a chair outside of the group didn't help. She'd go beserk, biting and scratching; she seemed to have a need for attention. She really likes other children." When I commented on the difficulty of Raina's adapting to a Montessori structure, which perhaps was different from her home structure, Teacher Jackie replied, "Well, they have to know the limits of different places."

I subsequently discovered that Raina's parents had not had the child evaluated and had withdrawn her from the school.

In this Montessori classroom, children such as Raina, Molly, and Jomo, who wished to play instead of work, emerged as social deviants—as problems, symbols of incomplete social-ization. The goal of the Montessori socialization process was the internalization of the external normative structure, where work was viewed as the medium, the corollary of individual control. Within this structure, work and play were rigidly de-marcated and the children were denied the possibility of *their* play—of fashioning and transforming their environment.

This work-play dichotomy presents an interesting historical paradox. It was Marx who advanced the thesis that work is the mode basic to the development of the self. While "man" is of the world, he changes and transforms his world through his labor; hence man makes his own history through his work. Maria Montessori took a similar position in outlining her theory of the "sensitive periods"[5] and the application of the "fundamental lesson,"[6] but transposed this theory upon the life-world of the child, thereby creating a false dichotomy between work and play. Play that is meaningful, play that fashions and transforms the landscape of the child, becomes authentic labor in the very act of playing; hence, childhood as a life phase does not dichotomize the meaningful purposive human activity of "work-play" (see chapter 9, below), for the child works while playing and plays while working.

It is the adult world that has imposed this dichotomy on the young child's experiences. Thus in the Montessori landscape, where routinized tasks and a fetishism of procedure rituals are emphasized, the right to "play" has been eroded. When "work" becomes the reification of play, we see the origins of the bureaucratization of childhood.

This systematic negation of self-initiated play and the edu-cation toward conformity and docility leads to well-adapted children who obey the Montessori rules and display interest in "work" but little interest in "play." Spontaneity becomes subordinate to the need for calm, order, and discipline. Creativity is bounded by the unidimensional function of the "work" materials and the constraints of the environment. In-deed, the "sameness" of the work environment was a crucial element in the Montessori classroom throughout my visits. No pictures drawn by children hung on the walls, no art work adorned the shelves—all that was made was mechanically *un-*

done before the work process was considered complete. A child did not possess the "history making" power to influence her interpersonal environment, nor imprint herself upon the landscape, nor transform her spatial surroundings. The environment bore no marks of children, but was stamped with the mark of the Montessori adult.

In such a situation the untrained active, playful, vigorous, mischievous toddler is construed as a problem because playfulness, physical activity, mischief, are *anti-norms* detrimental to the status quo of the school. We thus witness the manner in which differences are made pathological. The transgressors become the deviants of the institution; deviants who in another environment might be perceived as bright, imaginative, "normal" two-year-olds. The dialectical relativity of categorical constructs of "normalcy" and "deviancy" becomes evident after we have explored the existential landscape of these labeled children.

I now turn to a consideration of the Montessori Method as it pertains to classroom curriculum and consider its implications for learning from the perspective of Piaget's theory.

The Montessori Method—a Piagetian Critique: Play vs. Work

Most children in the toddler classes were in the sensorimotor stage of development or the early months of the preoperational stage—a stage characterized by extreme egocentrism, incipient classification operations, and a need for action-oriented activity. Piaget, in fact, views this action-centered stage as vital for later conceptual development; for it is action that forms the basis of thought.[7]

Symbolic representation and symbolic play are characteristics of this developmental stage, during which the child attains the slow glimmer of distinction between fantasy and reality. On a number of occasions, children in the classroom would engage in interactive, noisy fantasy play. Consider the staff response.

> Teacher Jackie observed Kyle and Alan shouting and laughing in the corner of the classroom, involved in imitating animals. She went and told Alan, "Please push your

chair in first." Kyle: "We playing." Teacher Jackie: "Are
you all done?" Kyle: "I play with Alan." Teacher Jackie: "Is
this your work Alan?" She goes off and gets another chair
for him, but Alan wanders off.

Jimmy, Bruce, and Sharon ran around the room, shouting
and laughing, and chasing each other. Teacher Martha:
"Jimmy, let's see if we can find some work for you to do";
and she led him off. Soon she returned to separate Sharon
and Bruce in similar fashion.

The implication underlying the teachers' intervention was
that *play is not legitimate;* hence in this environment a dichotomy between play and work was created. The antiplay
normative orientation militated against the developmental
function of play, which Piaget viewed as a medium for helping
the child assimilate experience to her personal schema of the
world. In addition, Bruner's studies on the functions of play
indicate that even the simplest play activities, far from being
random, are structured and governed by child-rules—that play
is the forerunner of adult competencies involving both
problem-solving ability and creativity.[8]

In analyzing the Montessori Method we notice a self-
defeating pattern: on the one hand, an emulation of work, a
prizing of the "absorbent mind," an elaborate attempt to
create original materials, and, on the other, a paradoxical denial of those natural processes which Montessori considered
vital for the child's growth. The source of this contradiction
lies in the latent ideology of containment where the environment is designed to produce a system of tight controls. Work is
merely the mode through which these controls are applied.
Once again we observe a stark discontinuity between educational philosophy and educational practice.

Work and Its Unidimensionality

But there is no freedom allowed the child to create.
He is free to choose which apparatus he will use,
but never to choose his own ends, never to bend
a material to his own plans. For the material is
limited to a fixed number of things which must be
handled in a certain way.[9]

Within this school, very little opportunity for active manipulation of the world of objects was provided. Each set of materials had one designated function, and no flexibility was permitted in terms of imaginative reconstruction of materials.

> Perry took the barrels and built a high tower, which tottered and fell on the floor. Perry laughed, picked up the barrels (upon instruction from Teacher Jackie), and tried to rebuild the tower. Teacher Jackie went up and told him the barrels were for screwing, not building, and proceeded to demonstrate how one operated the barrels. "This is tttightening. This is llllooser." Perry, not interested in screwing the barrels, threw them on the floor. Teacher Jackie instructed him very quietly to pick them up and put his work away.

Once again we observe the limitation on the child's desire to experiment with objects in the environment.

Many "work"-related activities were developmentally inappropriate to the children; however, drilling and rote learning formed a common pattern when children did not respond as expected.

> During circle time (the last half hour), one of the teachers would hold up name cards and children would be asked to identify their own names and then the names of others. The children's own names were called and initial consonants were accentuated. "Pppaul, Bbbenji, Sssandi." Children would imitate the teacher and shout their own name out, when asked to "read" the name card (i.e., every name is mine—displaying characteristic egocentrism). After about three to four months of repetition, children would begin to recognize their own names.

> During circle time, Teacher Jackie read the "Up and Down" book. A picture of a feather would be presented with corresponding adjective "light" and that of a rock with the adjective "heavy." Children would be asked to respond "heavy" or "light" when they saw the picture. However, the typical response was always a shouting out of the *noun*, not the *adjective*.

In the observation above, the children were responding to the concrete, to naming the world, rather than identifying abstract qualities verbalized by an adjective.

When the children did not spontaneously indicate a desire

to learn what was developmentally inappropriate, they were drilled to produce the correct response.

The emphasis in the school was on learning the correct procedure. Every action belied a unidimensional response as pointed out earlier in Dewey's critique. This pertained as much to the utilization of materials as to the mode of behavior in the work environment.

> Celia played with an eraser, banging it on the blackboard and watching the haze of dust emerge with each bang. Teacher Martha went up to her and explained, "This is how we use the eraser. Uppp, dddown, uppp, dddown."

We remember too Molly's chalk experiment with her toes and Perry's building of the tower. In these instances, the monofunctionality of the materials was stressed, and no allowance was made for flexible reconstruction. The stress on the correct use of materials and the exact manner in which the work was to be used created an orientation to "procedure learning" and a fetishism about rituals of correctness. Involvement with the materials was subordinate to the "taking out" and "putting away" procedures. We thus observe the rapid internalization of an external locus of "object" order on the part of the toddlers—with very little freedom to experiment freely with the world or to understand a world beyond exact procedural rituals.

The "learning environment" consonant with Montessori philosophy was, in large part, devoid of both positive and negative reinforcement.

> Bruce sat at a table with barrels. He counted 1, 2, 3, 4, 5, 6, 7, 8, 9, 10, stopped, looked around, and clapped himself. He repeated the counting, and three children joined in the self-applause. Both teachers looked on *without responding* and told the other three to move away.

> During circle time, the teachers sang "Little River Flowing to the Sea." As the song ended, Heather began to sing, "Twinkle Twinkle Little Star," remembering almost all of the words. When she finished, she stated, "I sing good." She looked around and repeated, "I sing good." No one replied.

The lack of praise and warm approval for spontaneous cognitive feats was extended into the social realm. Staff were seldom physically warm to the children. Children who cried were frequently left alone when words failed to soothe them. Teachers would try persistently to involve children in work when upset, and rarely would a child be spontaneously hugged or kissed. Holding a child was frequently a form of control rather than an act of close affection (recall Molly and the teachers' laps).

While up to this point I have sketched a detailed portrait of the lives of the youngest children in this institution, I now wish to briefly describe the preschool and kindergarten programs.

The Preschool Classroom

The norms of the preschool were essentially the same as its toddler counterpart, but there was less rigorous enforcement and less emphasis on the procedural order of the materials. This was not due to a more flexible orientation on the part of the staff but was, rather, dependent on two factors: (a) many of the children in the preschool had already attended the Montessori toddler class, and (b) the children were older, so that the training period for new arrivals was briefer and more manageable.

The ground rules of the school were described to me by Teacher Wanda.

> "No running in the classroom. No talking until you raise your hand when in the circle. All work must be replaced on the shelf after pushing in your chair . . . Taking turns on the line . . . helps to develop an awareness of the other . . . Children need to develop concentration before they can begin to develop in a self-aware way . . . When kids are able to concentrate, they can do *serious* work, not move around aimlessly."

The work ethic in the preschool still assumed paramount importance; children were now defined as successful through their work involvement.

"Yesterday Jerry was self-directed, not dispersed, because I kept him going from task to task."

Teacher Sandy informed me during one visit that a child, Katie, "has emotional problems. She has trouble getting into work . . . and making decisions."

The children interacted in groups far more than in the toddler class, but always centered their interactions around "work." Each table was designed for two children with a red line taped down the center. It was acceptable for children to "work" together, but not to "play" together. Any loud, noisy, exuberant "play" was seen to stem from lack of work involvement, and children were then encouraged "to find some work to do."

Children in these preschool classes tended to engage in more interpersonal conflict, and the staff handled the conflictful occurrences by separating the children, remonstrating in soft, calm tones, and sending them off to find work.

Teacher Wanda saw one child hit an onlooker in the library corner. The onlooker squealed. Teacher Wanda jumped up and ran over, saying quietly but incredulously to the aggressor, "Excuse me. What's happening? Please go and find work somewhere else."

A tussle between two children occurred over a particular piece of work. Teacher Wanda: "What's wrong, can you tell me? Why are you angry? You don't have work to do."

In the above interventions, Teacher Wanda spoke in a manner that I found maddeningly calm, quiet, apparently pitying the children's transgressions and astonished by their actions. I found their actions fairly typical of four- and five-year-olds. The incredulity of Teacher Wanda's reaction tended to convert an ordinary experience into an abnormal one. We notice here the reemergence of a social concept of abnormality and deviance created by inappropriate or "abnormal" norms.

When I enquired about the specific incidence of conflict, it was traced to a number of "troubled" or "problem" children. In Teacher Wanda's class, Sam and Farhad (Black and Asian children, respectively) were mentioned.

"Sam has some good and some bad days. When he goes around striking people, the children do not strike him back. They know he's troubled. I often say to the children, 'Sam is troubled today.'"

"Farhad cannot express himself in words . . . hard to understand him . . . he talks in a low, mumbly way. I try and get him to verbalize his anger."

Sam was subjected to an insidious labeling process in which his peers were encouraged to perceive him within a problem-oriented, "unwell," disease paradigm. The teachers and "adapted" children represented sanity, while Sam formed the deviant antithesis to the structure. Farhad, a foreign child who spoke with an accent, was more physical than verbal and was perceived as having a language and expression problem because the accepted mode of communication within the structure was verbal, not physical.

In summary, my impression upon entering this Montessori preschool classroom was one of amazement that thirty children and four teachers were contained in such an orderly fashion within a relatively small area; yet one did not experience the spatial restrictions very readily as the space was geared not to mobility but to sedentary activity. Whenever the spatial boundaries were transgressed, tight controls were exerted. I realized that the room, viewed as a school classroom, was not at all unusual. But what I had expected was space, openness, and mobility for two- to five-year-olds. My assumptions about the nature of childhood led me to conceive of a preschool as a spatially open area, not a spatially closed area. However, if one saw Montessori as a school classroom and not as a children's play area, certain redeeming features emerged. There were no rectangular rows of desks but, in fact, more internal space, as all materials were ranged on the periphery of the rectangular room. The director and staff viewed Montessori as an alternative to the public school system. Learning was individualized; there was free but contained movement; quiet talking was permitted; group work was permitted; there were no exams, etc. However, the question then arose whether such an alternative should be developed for preschoolers and toddlers. If one accepted the inevitability of schooling in the elementary years, did that provide a rationale for the early institutionalization and containment of very young children?

The director described the philosophy and goals of the school as follows:

> "To build an interest in exploring and learning, the acquiring of basic skills, the most important time in a child's life is early childhood to the end of kindergarten. We try to provide a preschool class of superior quality—use the classroom and teacher as resources." The director also stated that he believed there was a qualitative difference between Montessori preschoolers and others. "They tend to be a lot better able to express emotions and interact."

The Montessori school staff clearly saw themselves as creating an effective alternative education structure which better prepared children "to function in the larger society." The school, through its socialization process, could claim, perhaps, that its miniworkers were better *fit*, better *adapted* to function as future workers in a school system.

But the routinization of procedure and the maintenance of the internal equilibrium of the structure transposed upon the landscape of the child, in *all* the programs at this center, involved a systematic negation of freedom of exploration. Here the child was denied the power to invent because of the ascribed unidimensionality of the materials. To be creative, then, was actually to be subversive of the social order of this minibureaucracy.[10] The transposition of an adult-defined "work" world upon the child's landscape introduced false dichotomies between work and play and imposed an alien ideology upon the being of childhood. The child, to survive in such an institution, must be acculturated into a work ethic where productivity, efficiency, and conformity are perceived as synonymous with healthy development. To display interest in play and exploration, or merely to have a little bit of boisterous fun, testifies to the maladjustment of the individual child who fails to "be productively." When viewed through this lens, a Montessori educational experience thus becomes a training ground for the early bureaucratization of children.

6
Lollipop
Learning Center, Inc.

Lollipop Learning Center is a profit-run daycare corporation owned and operated by a husband-and-wife team. At present, four centers are operating in two counties, with the possibility of further expansion. The largest of these centers, situated in the central shopping area of a small city, offers full-time daycare and a part-time nursery program. The building in which the center is located is a small, split-level structure comprising a large basement, several small classrooms, an office, and a tiny outside play area (fifteen by thirty-five feet) bordered by a parking lot.

The approximately seventy children in daycare, ranging from two to six years old, are subdivided into two age groups of thirty to thirty-five children each. Described by the directors as the children of working mothers, they are predominantly from low-income and single-parent families.

The nursery school offers a part-day program "with a more cognitive emphasis," which is considerably more expensive than the daycare. The children that attend this program, numbering ten to twenty children per age group, are drawn mainly from middle-income or professional families where the mothers do not work. A small number of the nursery children move into daycare for the afternoon. There are very few black children in the nursery school; most tend to be heavily concentrated in the daycare classes.

This center is run by the male director, Mr. Smith. His wife, a certified preschool teacher, spends most of her time supervising one of the out-of-town centers, which offers an extended nursery school program. The downtown center, which forms the basis for the case study in this section, has one

certified nursery school teacher in addition to several assistants, aides, and high school students. The nursery school
children spend much of their time in the art and project room,
while a number of other classrooms are utilized for TV viewing, stories, "free play," and games. The basement hall is used
for large motor activity and snacks. The daycare children
utilize these same spatial areas on a rotating basis, but have
only secondary access to the art room and basement.

Childcare and the Profit Motive

"We're a privately owned corporation now and we
run independently . . . I was in the banking business
before this and daycare is a good business." (As
told to me by Mr. Smith during one of our early
meetings at the center.)

Many characteristics of Lollipop Learning Center were influenced by its underlying profit orientation and corporate
structure.

Space and Time

The experience of space was demarcated by the exigencies of
a rotating time schedule devised by Mr. Smith. As there were
approximately one hundred children present in the building
at one time, each group was allotted certain spatial areas during specific time periods. These space and time constrictions
were considered necessary in order to organize and control
the large numbers of children within the limited spatial area of
the school.

As Mr. Smith enrolled the maximum number of children
possible, received differing payments from nursery and daycare families, and staggered the attendance of the nursery
school children between morning and afternoon, he was
thereby able to obtain a maximum enrollment, ensure that the
school was filled to capacity, and, through spatial rotation,
meet the licensing code requirements. While receiving a rapid
turnover of profit, he paid a relatively low rent for the build-

ing, which was not equipped to handle the diversity of numbers.

When questioned about minority and ADC children (approximately 10 percent), Mr. Smith replied he was not in favor of ADC as "we lose money on those kids."

As space and time restrictions were related to profitable and maximum utilization of what was available, it became evident that space and time were resources to be utilized instrumentally without due consideration of the existential impact upon the day-to-day experience of the children.

As I entered the school this morning, thirty three-year-old daycare children were sitting cross-legged, lining the wall of the corridor outside the art room. The noise was deafening. Children were screaming, crying, and hitting each other. The three teacher aides stood by impassively and did not intervene. One little girl lay on the floor sobbing and calling, "Mama, Mama," but no one took any notice of her. As the nursery children emerged from the art room, the daycare children stood up and rushed in, shouting and pushing each other.

After snack time, the four-year-old daycare children stood in a line waiting to go into the art room. The noise level was very high. Children were running up and down, there was fighting, and the boys were punching each other. The male teacher was shouting at the children to "keep in your line," and "quit that," but he could hardly be heard. At that moment Mr. Smith walked by with a visiting parent. The noise subsided as he explained to the mother, "It's a bad day today. These children are waiting. The nursery school is meant to be out of there by 10:30." He called to one of the little boys and said, "C'mere, let me tie your laces." He fixed the child's shoe, patted his stomach and said, "You're a nice boy, Sam; I like you."

At each observation visit, I perceived this pattern of "corridor waiting." In most instances, the daycare children would form the waiting line, as both nursery school classes had primary access to the art and project room, and, in fact, usually utilized it until 10:45 A.M.

Frequently, activities would be abruptly interrupted by Mr. Smith, who played the role of timekeeper and "corridor supervisor."

As I entered the art room, an art activity was still in progress. The teacher aide looked at her watch and told the children to wash their hands and line up. One little girl tried to complete her drawing. Aide: "Well, you'd better hurry up as they'll run off and leave you." Mr. Smith entered. "Lesley, you'd better hurry. There's another group coming in and you'll get left behind." Lesley stood up, was taken to have her hands washed as the other group rushed in. Her project was taken off the table and she did not manage to complete it.

I found it interesting that the teachers and aides of both the nursery school and daycare continually ordered the children to march in line from one room to another. However, while the nursery school children always marched in an orderly, straight line, without speaking, the daycare children would not march in line unless threatened by Mr. Smith. They largely ignored the instructions of their teachers, and tended to bolt from one room to another.

Another phenomenon emerged during these observations: the inability to relate to others in time. When one considers the fact that two-thirds of these children spent ten hours a day, five days a week, at the school, the need to form relationships with other significant adults becomes a critical issue. A great number of the children, particularly the two-and-a-half- to four-year-olds, tended to cling to the teachers and aides. Many cried for their parents during the day. However, despite the evinced need for significant attachment, the children were not able to form any long-term relationships with adults. This was due to the extremely rapid turnover of staff every semester. In one and a half years I observed six changes of staff in the daycare and five in the nursery school. When I explored this phenomenon through a series of follow-up interviews with former staff, one of the teachers told me:

> "We were always chronically understaffed. I hated working there, and most staff people feel similarly. The rapid turnover suits the Smiths financially, as they only paid us the minimum."

I subsequently discovered that certified nursery school teachers were appointed as assistants to Mrs. Smith for the first year, although she was rarely present and these teachers supervised their own classes. This classification placed them in a lower wage bracket and, since most left within the year, their rank never changed. None of the daycare staff was certified, and most were classified as teacher aides, although Mrs. Smith, whom they were listed as aiding, rarely spent any time at the downtown center. In this way the staff were paid at a minimum, and, on paper, regulations were met. When I enquired how Mr. Smith had managed to "cover up" so effectively, the same teacher replied:

> "He has connections with the state. He also knows when the people [i.e., inspectors] are coming to visit."

While an overt pattern of deception began to emerge, which I gradually became aware of and suspicious about, a covert issue lay beneath: How were the children being socialized into detachment? As they were unable to form meaningful relationships in time with any staff member, how, I wondered, did they perceive the world? They were separated from home fifty hours a week—an explicit detachment in itself—and yet there were no secondary attachments to compensate that were either intimate or constant. Did this create a configuration of a world where relationships did not last, a world of inconstancy and uncertainty and confusion? As it was impossible to question the children about this, I could only explore from an adult-centered perception how these children possibly restructured that experience of loss and "constant inconstancy." I noticed that the older daycare children were either hostile or indifferent to the teachers, while the younger children tended to struggle toward the formation of an attachment despite frequent rejection and subsequent departure on the part of the staff. As they moved through a series of changes of this nature, however, they became indifferent—adapted to uninvolvement—a strong factor, I believe, which contributed to the existential atmosphere of anomie within this school.

Space, Time and Containment

One of the problems encountered by the daycare staff in the school was effective management of large groups of children. This problem was integrally linked to the problem of mass daycare; for in attempting to house large groups of children with untrained, often uninterested staff, within a confined space that lacked adequate equipment and materials, the problem of organization and management was transformed to a strategy of containment. One of the most effective containment instruments was the TV set.

Both daycare groups spent morning and afternoon periods in the TV room each day during fall and winter.

> During November, I walked into the TV room after the aide *unlocked* the door. I found the room cold and bare. Twenty-five children lay on the bare floor in the darkened room watching "Sesame Street." There was a high noise level, which tended to obscure the high volume of the TV set. After a few minutes of viewing, children began to run around, shout, scream, and hit each other. The one aide supervising the children stood at the back of the room, seemingly impervious to the chaotic situation. I noticed that two children were screaming hard and that their screams drowned the sounds of the program. After almost a half hour, the aide looked at her watch and shouted, "Time to move on." She walked up to the TV, switched it off in the middle of a story and marched the children out to the art room.

> On another occasion, I tried to enter the TV room, which was, as usual, locked. Mr. Smith stopped me and said, "Oh, I have three- and four-year-olds in there. They arrived late and missed the field trip." When the three- and four-year-old daycare group arrived back an hour later, they were sent to the TV room while an aide went to prepare the art project. She later returned, saying to the other aide, "When you're ready, I'm ready." The aide abruptly switched off the TV without any explanation to the children, and told them to line up to go to the art room.

The TV performed a useful function in the school. It was a way of "killing time," of keeping the children confined in one spatial area for a certain time period. This, in turn, allowed the staff to plan the next activity in the art room. It was evident from the attitude of the staff toward the children that little, if any, consideration was paid to the needs or interests of the children. TV programs were switched off without prior warning, without any regard for the children's feelings. The insensitivity on the part of the staff toward the children was even more pronounced during the frequent situations of chaos that I encountered in the TV room and elsewhere. Aides did not intervene during escalating situations of violence. However, this nonintervention arose from apathy rather than from a philosophy of nonintervention; for when Mr. Smith was around, they swiftly rose to discipline the children.

The locked doors were symbolic of *containment*. Children were not allowed free movement to and from any classroom, yet they continually directed their energies toward *escape*.

As I knocked on the block room door, an aide opened it and I squeezed through the narrow space. Before I could close the door, two children ducked under my arm and ran out. The aide ran after them, grabbed them back and locked the door. When I rose and left a half hour later, the same attempted escape occurred, and the aide ran out trying to round up the children. As I stood in the corridor watching, I became aware that the sixteen children in the block room were unattended. I walked back in, and was witness to one child threatening to hit another with a heavy wooden truck, which I removed amid an almost deafening noise level: screaming, stomping, throwing of blocks, and thudding. I remained there for twenty minutes before any staff member reentered. When she returned, I myself ran out, experiencing a sense of relief. I left the school soon afterward with a splitting headache, filled with a sense of nausea.

I too was happy to escape from the room and school that day, and wondered if my experience at all resembled that of the children. They were contained within an atmosphere of chaos, confusion, and impersonality fifty hours a week. My biweekly visits left me feeling physically ill and shaken. I was struck by the fact that, after four months, I knew virtually no names of the daycare children. The aides seldom referred to children by name, and, because there were so many children, I could not keep my usual track of their individual personalities. They were not a group of individuals to me but an anonymous crowd; they did not even seem to know the names of their own peers. This impersonality and anonymity was a pervasive experience for me, which was not ameliorated by the passage of time.

The *insignificance* of the child within this "childcare" setting ran counter to the Smiths' description of their school:

> Mrs. Smith described the center as a "home away from
> home," and Mr. Smith stated that "the daycare serves par-
> ents by providing a warm, secure place for their children."

While the preceding descriptions have pertained almost exclusively to the daycare children, it is necessary to turn our
attention to the *differences* that existed between daycare and
nursery school children and to examine the social impact of
these differences.

Stratification and Exclusion

The nursery school was qualitatively different from the daycare. There was a lower ratio of children to adults, one to nine;
the program was more structured and only ran for three hours
each day. The children of the nursery school attended the
school *part-time;* they did not undergo an all-day "school" experience as did the daycare children. The nursery school children were better dressed, they had primary access to the art
room and equipment, their teachers were trained professionals, and they were given superior snacks. The common snack
of the nursery school children was baked goods as a school
project, or cookies and juice. The daycare children received
dry crackers and diluted juice!

The daycare children wore tags on their backs, identifying
them as such, emphasizing the strict division between the
nursery school and daycare children. Both groups of children
appeared to be aware of the divisions; the latter appeared to
feel strongly excluded, while the nursery school children
were self-consciously exclusive.

> One morning the three-year-old nursery school class was in
> the story room. Teacher: "Now, I want everyone to be quiet
> while I go out and get the stories, O.K.?" She departed, and
> a daycare child with a "DC" tag on his back came to the
> open door. The nursery school children shouted (in chorus),
> "Hey, you, get out of here; get out." Charles, the eldest,
> jumped up, pushed the child out, and slammed the door.

When the teacher returned, he said, "Teacher, I pushed a boy from daycare out of here." Teacher: "You did? We don't push here, do we."

Mr. Smith observed a little girl trying to enter the art room, where the nursery school children were busily making Halloween pumpkins. Mr. Smith: "Hey, you, this is the nursery school. Go back to the daycare group where you belong."

At mid-morning, the three-year-old daycare group returned to the building from a field trip. All twenty-seven children were lining the corridor, waiting to enter the art room. One child ran to the door and tried to enter. A second child shouted: "Hey, where you going? Get back here; you can't go in *there*." At that point the nursery school teacher opened the door and said, "I'm sorry, you don't belong in here. Why don't you go and play outside?" She shut the door in the child's face, and he cried.

During snack time for the nursery school children, two daycare children were sitting eating lunch from their lunchboxes at another table in the basement. Mr. Smith walked in with a visiting mother and child. He walked up to the children and said loudly, and with simulated affection, "What are you eating lunch for; it's not lunchtime," and walked off smiling and winking at the visiting mother while telling the daycare children to go upstairs. The daycare children continued to sit there as he left, and the nursery school teacher served the banana bread that the group had made, saying, "Is it good? Are we good cooks?" The daycare children sat silently watching the children eat. After a while the teacher, noticing them, handed them two end pieces with honey. They nodded thank you and ate up the leftovers.

The latter observation was a striking, poignant, and rather typical example of the *differences* in treatment between nursery school children and daycare. Not only did the daycare children form the deprived class in this school, they also appeared to be aware of their inferior status. Snacks were always a treat for the nursery school, and daycare children would, on occasion, sneak down to the basement and attempt to partake of the nursery school snacks, which meant eating the leftovers. Mr. Smith's reaction in the above instance was *atypical*. I was surprised by his jovial attitude and seeming gentleness; for only a few weeks previously I had witnessed another snack time, when Mr. Smith, perceiving a similar daycare transgression had shouted:

> "Hey, what are you kids up to? Get out of here then; you don't belong here. You, too, and you . . ."

The children's own attitudes toward the nursery school and daycare indicated the manner in which they restructured the "exclusive-excluded" experience. The nursery school was ascribed a higher, more positive status, while the daycare was ascribed a lower, negative status. As we have noted, the nursery school children were aware of some form of separateness and attempted to exclude a child on the basis of his being a "daycare kid." Daycare children, on the other hand, frequently attempted to *burst into* the nursery school, only to experience exclusion and rejection. The fact that many of the daycare children were from low-income families, were black, or were members of other minority groups, produced a stratification system that mirrored the reality of the macrosocial structure. The stratification system existed among the staff members, too. The nursery school teachers looked down on the daycare staff, the latter being untrained and non-professional; and the daycare staff, who worked longer hours than the nursery school staff, resented receiving less pay. There was no contact, to my knowledge, between these two groups during the school day other than a formal greeting as they rotated past each other from room to room.

One of the teachers described her feelings about daycare as follows:

> "I felt very badly for the kids I wasn't teaching [i.e., daycare] . . . when my nursery school kids had to stay on for lunch with daycare. They cried; they were scared. When you're locked up all day, you'd be that way too." (Extracted from an interview after this teacher, too, had left the school.)

The Children of Violence

Violence is a symptom. The disease is variously
powerlessness, insignificance, injustice—in short, a
conviction that I am less than human and I am
homeless in the world.[1]

The fragmentation of physical space and the dislocation of
social space and time resulted in fragmented interpersonal
relationships. Children were alienated from their peers and
from their teachers. The staff, in turn, were alienated from
each other. This alienation produced a social landscape of
pervasive anomie which may well have scarred the lives of
some of these children. Children were the pawns of a relent-
less enterprise. While they, in fact, were responsible for making the enterprise work (i.e., their parents were the consumers), they were alien to the culture of the school; for it was
not a child-centered culture, nor even an adult-centered culture dedicated to the socialization of children, such as we observed in Golda Meir Nursery and Busy Bee Montessori. The
most telling factor about this school was that *children did not
matter existentially. They mattered instrumentally.* The children were the instruments of an institution dedicated to material gain and profit, not to childcare, nor to education. The
social ramifications of this dehumanizing system were evident
in the violent internal structure, a violence that was perpetuated between teacher and child and among peers. One of
the common manifestations of teacher violence was in the
form of *scapegoating.* Within each class, in both the nursery
school and daycare, certain children were constantly reprimanded, punished, or, in some cases, humiliated by the staff.
These children were predominantly black. They were also the
children whose names I was likely to know, as they were
labeled the troublemakers. The two children that I had observed as "troublemakers" in the nursery school were, after a
period of time, shifted to daycare. When I enquired of Mr.
Smith why Vera—a bright, lively three-year-old black
child—had been moved out of the nursery school, he replied,
"Oh, she was very manipulative, a problem child."

The following extracts are selected from biweekly records of
so-called "troublemakers."

Jimmy was sitting next to an aide in the TV room. Aide: "Now everyone switch off your mouths and turn on your ears." Jimmy cried out, "Eeeeeee." The aide grabbed his mouth. "You don't scream." He defiantly screamed, "Eeeeeee," again. She pushed him off his chair and said to the second aide, "He can't listen. Take him out." The child resisted, shouting, "No, no." The aide: "If you don't, she'll take you out." The aide then began a story about ABC. The room was extremely noisy; children were running around, screaming, hitting, and punching each other. Jimmy, one of the many children running around, was grabbed. "Now you had your chance." He began to scream, and the aide unlocked the door and *threw* him out. She closed and locked the door. She continued to read the story, although no children were listening and many were crying or shouting. I later found out that Jimmy had been found by Mr. Smith on his corridor patrol and taken to the office.

During a visit to the wooden block room I observed the male assistant teacher sitting at a table tapping a tune with his fingers, seemingly a spectator to an almost deafening uproar in the room. After a few minutes he stood up and walked around. One child, Jack, sat on a large wooden truck and tried to ride it. Teacher: "Hey, I told you not to sit on it; leave the room." The child began to cry and lay down. Teacher to another child: "Well, I guess Jack's dead; you can have his blocks now!"

Two regular activities occurred in the four-year-old daycare apart from TV viewing. One of those was "free play" and "building" in the block room, and the other was the game "Blind Man's Bluff." At each visit I witnessed this game being played out, directed by the above teacher.

Two boys were blindfolded, and the teacher issued instructions. "Get your hands out. O.K., you guys, you've got to freeze." The children, however, would not freeze, and moved away as the blindfolded boys approached. The teacher took Shawn, a black child who moved, to the corner. "If you don't like that, play the game properly." He then picked on another child (one of the four who moved), once again, black, and said, "Coleman, if you move again, you're going to sit down and that's going to be the end of it. O.K., Coleman, sit down. I told you to listen and you didn't."

The images of this game were interesting. The object of the game was for the two blindfolded children to catch the "seeing" children, who, however, were required to freeze when the order was issued. However, to the children, this seemed to indicate that they should allow themselves to be caught, whereas their first response was to escape. The game worked on the basis of *entrapment*, and the children refused to be entrapped. This refusal, however, resulted in punishment by their teacher. The game assumed a ritualistic symbolism over the two-year period of observation; for it lent an archetypal significance to the reality of the day, and suggested a fundamental struggle between the desire of the child trying to escape, and the role of the teacher trying to contain the child within the locked rooms.

Scapegoating and the Public Humiliation of Coleman

Today, as I entered the "Blind Man's Bluff" game room, I witnessed an ugly incident. Coleman was standing in the center of the room with his head down, sobbing. Next to him was a puddle of urine. The male assistant teacher shouted at him and called him "a stupid baby." The other children joined in and began to laugh at him. The teacher ordered Coleman to fetch a mop from the bathroom "and mop up your own pee." Coleman wept bitterly as he did this, and afterward he was told to stand in a corner with his back to the class as punishment. The child looked devastated. His face was streaked with tears, and he would not take his eyes off the floor. My heart went out to him, and I experienced a strong surge of anger coupled with a feeling of helplessness.

When I later enquired of the above staff member what had happened, he replied that Coleman should have gone to the bathroom earlier when the others had. I found it hard to believe that a four-and-a-half-year-old child would have "just peed" without being subjected to some prior form of provocation or fear—particularly as Coleman was one of the liveliest children in the class and, hence, a frequent target of teacher anger. However, I never discovered what *did* happen earlier that morning.

The phenomenon of scapegoating occurred in a more covert and less violent fashion in the nursery school. Once again, however, the difficult children happened to be black.

> After project time was completed, at approximately 10:15, the nursery school children were required to take fifteen-minute "naps" on towels on the tiled floor. Vera refused to lie down on her towel on the floor. Teacher: "Vera, you're going to have a lot of room by yourself; here we go," picked her up and carried her to the other side of the classroom. Vera kicked and struggled. Teacher: "Vera, sit down. Vera, I asked you to sit down." By this time, a number of other children were standing too. The teacher ignored the others and continued to reprimand Vera. "Would you rather go to the office with Mr. Smith?" Vera obeyed and sat down.

As mentioned earlier, Vera was later transferred to daycare, being considered a "problem child" in the nursery school.

While scapegoating and teacher violence were common features of this school, the children, in turn, appeared to internalize this institutional violence and unleash it upon their peers. The level of physical aggression, violent acts, hostility, and often random attacks on classmates was unparalleled in any other school I observed. The situation, during most periods of the daycare, resembled chaos juxtaposed with attempts to maintain rigid order with threats and punishment.

Perhaps the most extreme manifestation of inter-child violence was to be found in the four-year-old daycare, which for eight months had been supervised by the male assistant teacher mentioned previously. That was the most chaotic class I visited and also the class in which the children were the most subjugated. The children were afraid of Douglas and cowed by his authority. Shortly after he left, a young woman teacher took over the group, and the following extract describes the class after a month's experience with their new teacher, Nellie.

> Teacher Nellie appeared self-conscious and suspicious of me at our first meeting. She told me that the "kids are unusually wild today." Kids were fighting each other, using assorted makeshift weapons—a baseball bat, a wooden pole, wooden blocks, plastic trays were all being thrown *at* the other children. Teacher Nellie continually shouted,

"Stop it," but no one took any notice. She dragged two children out of the room, pushed one into a corner, and ran back to switch off the lights as the basement turned to near chaos. One boy hit another on the head with a baseball bat. The environment was dangerous. I was hit twice by flying tennis balls and ducked to avoid a baseball bat. I noticed Coleman beating up other children, hitting one on the head with a truck, and pummeling and punching another. When he noticed me, he came up and asked me, "Would you stay all day?" and "Will you come back another day?" I told him I would, and he spoke to me for a few minutes. When the children were told to line up for the TV room, he seemed to randomly attack two other children who began to cry. He was sent to the back of the line. As the children walked out, four were screaming and one little girl was holding her head.

When I left the school that day, I reflected upon Sartre's prophetic words in his preface to Frantz Fanon's *Wretched of the Earth:* "We have sown the wind; he is the whirlwind. The child of violence at every moment he draws from it his humanity."[2] While I had been witness to a whirlwind phenomenon, witness to the children of violence recreating a violence among themselves, were they drawing authenticity and humanity from their actions, in history-making time, as Sartre believed the Algerian native had? I doubted it. I saw instead a gradual disintegration of shared child bonds, an erosion of play, a growing tide of alienation and social dislocation, an atmosphere of smoldering resentment and anger directed more frequently toward peers than toward the perpetuators of the cycle of violence—the staff. Within this school, over an extended period of time, I had been witness to the growth and development of an unremitting and severe form of social anomie which was to taint the early lives of these children and perhaps take its toll far beyond childhood.

While involved in the process of observation and subsequent exploration of the nature of the social landscape of this school, I searched for an area of positive contribution; I attempted to look for redeeming features. After many months, it became unquestionably clear to me that the social environment was destructive, that the lack of care and affective involvement was detrimental to the lives of these children.

However, if the school served no positive social purpose, I wondered, did it perhaps contribute in the cognitive domain? Was there anything of value in the learning environment that could perhaps justify the school's existence on the basis of preschool educational criteria?

The Cognitive Learning Environment

In this section, it is necessary to make a distinction between the curriculum of the daycare and nursery school. Hence, I propose to discuss each separately.

The Learning Environment of the Daycare

As the daycare children had only secondary access to the cognitive spatial areas, and the shifting daycare staff were untrained, apathetic workers, there was no developed curriculum. Instead, the daycare activities tended to shadow the themes of the highly structured nursery school. This lent a semblance of order and continuity to the otherwise disorganized day.

Much of what the staff aides attempted to "teach" to the children was crudely inapplicable to their developmental level or did not capture their interest. TV was considered "educational"; during fall and winter, the daycare children watched "Sesame Street" daily.

> One morning the children were marched into the darkened TV room, and "Sesame Street" was switched on. One child cried and said, "But I don't want to watch." The teacher aide replied, "Well, here's a book; look at that," and threw a book at the child as she proceeded to switch off the one remaining light. I wondered how the child was expected to look at a book in the dark!

Each day, stories were read to the children with a "cognitive lesson"; however, the books were old and dull. None of the current popular storybooks were available. The aides could not read fluently; some could not read at all, and those who could, frequently read in a monotone. The children were required to sit still and keep quiet.

"Now I want you all to keep your mouths closed while I'm reading the story"; the aide proceeded to read a book about apples and corresponding numbers. No participation by the children was invited and questions were silenced. The children fidgeted and ran around; and within a few minutes, fighting and screaming broke out.

During story time for the three-year-old daycare, one aide attempted to read a book while two others patrolled the room, which was in near chaos. Two children were hitting each other, two were screaming, and three or four were running around trying to escape the aide. The following material was read by the aide. She showed the children a picture of a coffee pot adjacent to a drum and asked, "Is the coffee pot a drum?" No one answered. The aide replied: "No. Is this (pointing to a drum) a drum? Yes. Why? Because he pounds on it. Is a house a parkbench? No. Why? Because you can't sit on it. Buttered toast is not a toy. Do you think it is a toy? No. Why? Because you can't play with it."

The above conversation was conducted as an entire monologue, in which the aide both asked and responded to her own absurd questions. It appeared that the "lesson" was designed to teach children to discriminate objects by their function and to label objects correctly. However, the analogies and defining functional qualities were ludicrous and were oriented to unidimensional, rigid definitions. The children were clearly *not* captured by the lesson and were inattentive and bored.

Process vs. production. During the time allotted to the art and project room, the daycare children were passively involved in the production of artifacts. No attention was paid to the child's *involvement in the process of doing.* On a number of occasions, I observed the aides making elaborate turkeys (Thanksgiving), decorations (Christmas), valentines, etc., while the children were given subsidiary activities such as drawing or clay to occupy them. Each artifact was labeled with a child's name, and the child would usually be called up for a token finishing touch to the product, which would then be taken home or used to adorn the corridor.

When I entered the art room today, the noise level was deafening. One aide was handing out *one* sheet of white paper to each child. She wrote the name of each child on the back of the paper. One broken crayon was dropped in front of each child. They were told to draw, while the two aides sat in a corner making wire animals, each of which bore the name of a daycare child. Soon, the children began to grab each other's crayons and fight over the colors. One of the aides said, "If you want another color, trade with your neighbor." A half-filled box of crayons lay unused on the table next to the aide.

The children could not experiment with many different drawings as they were given only one piece of paper, which was labeled as theirs. Neither were they free to create a drawing of different colors, as they were only given one crayon. I wondered why each child had not been given a selection, as there were plenty remaining in the box. Children were not encouraged to share but to trade when conflict arose. The method and vocabulary of the marketplace was present, and the children fought over the scarce resources, i.e., the crayons. They were also encouraged to compete with one another; most projects were prefaced by: "Let's see who can make the best picture today. Let's see who can finish first today."

The Learning Environment of the Nursery School

The nursery school, in contrast to the daycare, was efficiently organized, highly structured and followed a preplanned curriculum. The following is an outline of the four- to five-year-old nursery school schedule:

8:45 – 9:45	Art/project activities
9:45 – 10:15	Block room and "free play"
10:15 –10:45	Snacks, movement, reading readiness, French (in basement)
10:45 –11:15	Outside/movement and games (in basement)

The younger nursery school group followed a similar routine while utilizing the space at different intervals, and being required to take a fifteen-minute "nap" prior to snack time.

The curriculum was geared to the development of "early"

cognitive skills, and to this end, children were given daily "reading readiness" lessons and conversational French three times a week. Both of these cognitive lessons were taught through the traditional medium of repetition, drilling, and rote learning.

Each week the curriculum was built around a theme, usually reflecting the rituals or festivities of the larger society.

The pumpkin project. In the younger (three- and four-year-old) nursery class, the teacher handed out white pumpkin outlines and asked the children to identify the shape. Most children responded "apples," but Reggie said, "pumpkins for Halloween." Teacher: "Very good, Reggie." She gave out orange paint and brushes. "But first we've got to put your names on." The procedure of name writing and paint mixing took ten minutes, and the children sat quietly until they were given permission to paint. They were told to paint only the inside. "Now, let's get to work and let's make it all orange." Vera (previously described as a problem child by Mr. Smith and later transferred to day-care) took the paper and turned it into a hat, which she put on her head. Teacher: "That is not what we do, Vera. Please keep the paper on the table." The other black child in the class, Shawn, painted the outside of the circle with his fingers. Teacher: "Come on, Shawn, don't make a mess. You paint on the paper with the brush, not with your fingers." The teacher praised the children who did as they were told by saying, "Oh, good job. Oh, Charles, you're such a good worker,. You're doing real nice." While the children were occupied, the teacher was busy making elaborate pumpkin collages, to which the painted-in pumpkin outline was later attached, and the completed project was labeled with each child's name, respectively and sent home.

Turkeys for Thanksgiving. A month later, a new teacher took over this group and handed out white sheets of paper to the children while she worked on stuffed paper turkeys. The children were told to draw, and were called up individually to put the finishing touch (eyes) to an elaborately made turkey. Shawn drew a picture of an airplane, which was amazing in its shape and detail. His nose was running, and the teacher took out a kleenex. "Shawn, blow your nose, don't wipe it. I don't want it; throw it away" (in a distasteful tone). He tried to show her the airplane, but she took no notice. Shawn brought it to me, and I remarked, "What a great airplane. That's terrific." When she heard me, she turned around, and I said, "How old is Shawn?" She replied, "Three," and frowned. I remarked, "He's drawn a fantastic picture with terrific shape and perspective." She replied, "Oh, yes, Shawn loves that kind of thing." She then stood up and with a new seeming show of interest, "What did you make, Shawn?" Shawn looked up and seemed surprised and did not answer. She asked, "A house?" (It certainly did not look like a house!) Shawn repeated, "A house," almost mumbling. She said, "Oh very nice, Shawn," and went back to turkey making. I interrupted and said, "But Shawn told me it was an airplane with two propellers." Shawn overheard and said, "Yes, it's a house-airplane," and began pasting windows on the airplane.

I found it disturbing that in the following few months both Vera and Shawn were transferred to daycare. They both stood out in the nursery school class as bright and imaginative children. Shawn displayed particular talent in art work, which passed unnoticed. Both children were considered to be "disruptive" influences on the class, and I could understand why. Their creativity was anticonformist, and only conforming behavior was rewarded in the classroom. The conforming children were the "good workers" who did "good jobs."

It was clear, too, that the children's own experience, their own process of involvement, was subordinate to the product orientation of the teachers. Their experience was almost incidental to the job of producing artifacts. Activities for the children were not geared toward growth and learning, but rather to keeping the children occupied and docile while the teachers made the projects. Within this setting then, it was difficult to recognize creativity and imagination, for this constituted a structural deviation from the social order.

Herbert Gintis has remarked that "schools, by mirroring the impersonal and competitive relations of the corporate structure and the bureaucratic authoritarian aspects of alienated work, thwart the development of true initiative, independence and creativity in their charges. Thus, they attempt to produce docile unimaginative workers, filling the needs of hierarchical commodity production."[3] While the socializing function of the nursery school appeared to resonate with such assumptions, that of the daycare clearly did not. The disorganization, fragmentation, and anomie of the daycare did not produce "docile" workers but, rather, violent and disobedient non-workers. Hence, within a single school, a different social impact is observed. The nursery's function seems consonant with the socialization ideals and goals of the "schooling" process, but the daycare did not reflect this. Indeed, it was *dysfunctional*, tending to mirror the results of a corporate system gone amok, the extreme implications of an enterprise dedicated to the profit motive where the profit integers were not objects but children. The dehumanization that resulted from this instrumental ideology was not clearly visible to the casual observer. Sham and deception tended to conceal the core of these children's experiences, in which inner and outer realities were starkly divergent. My own experience as an "observer-participant" in this school was very different from all other "observer" experiences. Here I became an "uncoverer," an explorer into the ever-deepening gulf between the manifest and latent levels of reality.

The Phenomenon of Deception and Sham

Sham is related to distrust, which is, paradoxically, a form of belief—a belief in unreliability, a belief in the inimical. Sham is an expression of the metaphysic of the inimical and therefore embodies our feelings of vulnerability . . . It is characteristic of pathological social systems, whether countries, tribes, or families, that the inimical is imagined to be right inside the walls, and it is characteristic of many mad men that the inimical is felt to be inside their souls. Hence individually and socially, there are two "ideal" kinds of madness: that in which the inimical is felt to be outside and that in which it is felt to be inside. Corresponding to these are two forms of sham—one to mislead the outside enemy and another to deceive the inner.[4]

The public image that Lollipop Learning Center, Inc., presented to the community was, to a large extent, a positive one. There was a full enrollment throughout the year while other daycare centers in the area suffered "ups and downs." To an outsider, to a parent, to a casual observer, this center looked no better and no worse than other daycare centers. It had many practical advantages—it was a convenient location, ran a full day from 7:30 to 5:30, offered different types of programs, and required no parent participation whatsoever. As Mr. Smith remarked to me during an interview, "We don't want a whole lot of mothers telling us how to run the program."

Most other childcare centers required a minimum of parent participation on committees, involvement in maintenance, and, to differing degrees, token or active assistance on field trips or certain curricular activities. In this school the parents were, in toto, outsiders to their children's education and thus to their daily lives. This was convenient for many "working single parents" who did not want the responsibility of participation or lacked the "time" to devote to daycare involvement. Most parents made one visit before enrolling their child. As I was often present during the initial visit, I frequently witnessed the way in which the school was "sold" to the prospective customer. The times during which appointments were set up for parent visits were concentrated in mid-morning, when daycare children would be taken out of the building or to the basement, and nursery school children were busily engaged in projects.

My own initial entrance to the school was mediated by Mr. Smith, who during the midseventies was, as he put it, "still new to the business." At that time many of the statements he made to me smacked of naiveté. He seemed unaware of the implications of his utterances. Two years later he was far more proficient in childcare jargon and portrayed a different picture of the school, consonant with Mrs. Smith, a trained early childhood teacher.

As I became more and more a part of the landscape, I no longer had to preplan my visits weeks in advance. As a familiar figure, I gained more and more access to the real experience of the children. I was able to float in and out of the structure. As I offered no direct criticism, I believe Mr. Smith saw me as unthreatening; for he discouraged other observers during the same period. So I held a strange position in the structure, for I was no longer *noticed* as an observer. The fact that I was permitted to observe the internal reality made me wonder about the level of inner sham that existed for the directors. They knew, and I knew, that what they said in interviews was not true, yet they said it, and I wrote it down. Were they themselves so socialized into their own inner world of deception that they no longer saw the stark dichotomy between appearance and reality? Had they come to believe in their own pretence?

It was clear that external sham was functional, for it brought in the dollars and increased the profit. But what of the inner sham, the mode of inauthenticity that they moved through daily? I often wondered why they allowed me to continue visiting. *Were they not afraid of what I would see? Or did they themselves no longer see what was there?*

My own observations of the school sharply contradicted the stated goals and philosophy of the directors, as did the statements of former staff members. Several interview extracts are cited below in order to illustrate the gravity of the situation.

Extracts from Interviews with Mr. and Mrs. Smith

Mr. Smith

On A.D.C. "We lose money on those kids ... In the nursery school we have lots of doctors' kids and professional mothers. That's the way we like it—we get paid that way."

On discipline. "I believe in being firm with them. They listen to me because I'm a man. I don't have any trouble with them. There are four kids here who are troublemakers. I lock them in a separate room or put them in the office. Some of the gals do some hairpulling or spanking. I don't need to do it."

During this first interview with Mr. Smith, I believe that his frankness was due to a naiveté about the dos and don'ts of daycare, having only recently joined his wife as co-director of the newly opened corporation. The second interview, which took place eighteen months later, was of a different flavor.

"No spanking is allowed by the teachers. We try and encourage the kids to work out the problems for themselves. We talk about sharing; . . . all physical aggression is stopped immediately and both are disciplined."

On the function of the daycare and nursery school. "The daycare performs a great service to parents by providing a warm, secure place for children. We provide custodial care and try to teach them the basics, academically and socially, that they wouldn't get in babysitting.

"The nursery school has higher expectations—more cognitive. We teach them how to get along with others. It's more structured to prepare the kids for kindergarten. It's 75 percent academics."

On staff certification. "We need only one certified teacher in the building, but most of our aides are graduates anyway."

As we observe, Mr. Smith's statements on spanking were contradictory. It was *not* true that there was no spanking. Neither was it true that children were encouraged to work out problems themselves. I never observed any instances of that. His statements on staff certification were misleading and those about his aides, untrue. In reality, he was violating the licensing code requirements.

Mrs. Smith

On discipline. "We adopt the 'Let's talk about it' approach; teachers never jump in immediately. I'm very concerned about feelings—get their feelings out. No spanking or slapping of kids is allowed. We explain to kids why we don't allow this and always explain on the child's level."

On competition. "They love it and I foster it. They learn self-reliance and self-independence that way—that's why we're in school—keep on trying. Cooperation is fostered by competition, an esprit de corps. They learn that there are winners and losers, leaders and followers in life, but I always reward the losers for trying."

On the philosophy of the school. "We see ourselves as a home away from home, a substitute family, as we attract many one-parent families. We're a husband and wife team and try and

give a family feeling. We're the Momma and Daddy as positive models. If a child feels good about himself, he'll feel good
about learning"!

Extracts from Interviews with Former Staff Members

On the Smiths as directors. "They're in it for the money. The
school has nothing to do with daycare. It's really sick; and Mr.
Smith used to hit the kids."

On the organization of the school. "They don't put any money
back into it—no supplies, no staff increases. They pit staff
members against each other, so there was always staff conflict.
Everybody would say bad things about the Smiths, but no one
would back me up."

On the children. "The kids were always so crowded that they
would start to hit each other. There was a very high level of
aggression. *When you're locked up all day, you'd be that way
too. I could never stand the noise at the school—and the parents were unaware of what was going on!*"

The Childcare Business

As discussed earlier in this chapter, the defining structural
characteristic of Lollipop Learning Center was that it was a
childcare business geared to the profit enterprise. To what
extent is the resultant dehumanization, violence, and widespread anomie we have observed a feature of this very same
structural characteristic? It has become clear, as we have explored this institution's inner reality, that sham and deception
are used to mask widespread disregard for children. Children
are instrumental resources, parents are consumers, and the
product is frequently an abusive childcare system. The lives of
children are secondary to the profit motive, which dominates
spatial availability, time, staff services, children's experiences,
and the overall social and existential landscape.

Within this school we have viewed the development of a

stratification system which has mirrored the class structure
and division of labor within the macrosocial system. We have
noted an unremitting alienation and the disintegration of
shared interpersonal bonds. The level of inauthenticity has
been traced, as has the deficient cognitive environment.
Given the above configurations of "childcare," one needs
to question very critically this school's "rights of existence."

We need also question the growing increase of similar daycare centers predicated exclusively upon the corporate
paradigm and dedicated to the profit enterprise. These profit-
run centers have, too, expanded into franchised corporations,
and the *childcare industry* has become a relatively new, but
burgeoning, phenomenon in the United States. As early as
1970, Joseph Featherstone, writing for the *New Republic*,
raised the specter of "Kentucky Fried Children," for
businessmen, even then, were rushing to market franchises for
childcare "the way others have sold franchises for root beer
and fried chicken."[5]

The "National Institute of Education 1980 Report" indicates that 40 percent of the daycare centers in this country
are profit-run institutions.[6] Fortunately not all such centers
resemble Lollipop Learning Center; yet it is apparent that in
this area of daycare, children are at their most vulnerable to
exploitation. The extensive surveys conducted by Mary
Keyserling indicated findings disturbingly similar to my own.
Given the prohibitive costs of running a good center and the
need to keep fees reasonably low, Keyserling found that "at
best, good daycare is almost a non-profit commodity."[7]

Selma Fraiberg has sketched an ironic and sad portrait of the
powerlessness of the child in this burgeoning industry:

> As an industry, Child Care Industries Incorporated is in a
> unique position. Its services and personnel can range from
> "good" to "deplorable" and the consumer in the age range
> one month to six years will not write letters to the manage-
> ment regarding the quality of service. (Nor is he in a posi-
> tion to withdraw his patronage.) Since his parents are not
> really the direct consumers of the services rendered, they
> are rarely in a position to judge the quality. In other trades,
> this is known as a seller's market. The question for us is,
> "How fare the children?"[8]

Clearly, if "small facts speak to large issues," the lives of children at Lollipop Learning Center, Inc., stand in jeopardy, as do those of their brothers and sisters incarcerated in other such early childhood institutions across this country.

7

Martin Luther King
Childcare Center

Martin Luther King is a federally funded, low-income daycare center located in a downtown community building. The center bus transports the children to and from their homes, provides a cooked breakfast and hot lunch, and operates Monday through Friday from 7:30 A.M. to 5:30 P.M.

Approximately forty children between the ages of two-and-a-half and six attend the center full time, with the exception of the older children, who are transported there after attending the nearby public school kindergarten. The large second floor of the community building has been converted into the main preschool area with adjacent kitchen. Room dividers create three separate areas into which the children are loosely organized according to younger, middle, and older groupings. The basement contains heavy play equipment and cots, and is used for napping and movement activities. As the community building overlooks a busy main road, there is no playground, but there is a small enclosed cement patio which serves as an outside play area.

The population of the school is predominantly black with a few white and Chicano children. The black female director, Mrs. Tally, supervises several black teachers, only one of whom is actually certified while two others are enrolled in community college early childhood programs. In addition to numerous aides and volunteers of both sexes, there is the "grandmother program," which operates at a number of such centers, ensuring the daily presence of three grandmothers, two black and one white.

A substantial number of the children who attend this center have no "home" in the traditional sense of the word. Some are the casualties of poverty; others come from broken marriages, broken alliances, and a cycle of welfare insecurity, having been shunted from one living arrangement to another, often taken in by kindly friends or relatives. Some siblings have been split up, and a number of the children were underfed upon entry to the preschool. In the particular urban area in which these children lived, one did not find the traditional "extended family" in existence, which so often in the past has formed the bulwark of the poor and specifically, in this case, of lower-class black culture. The fragmentation and social dislocation of the urban poor within this area and the lack of community were perceived as problems by the director. Hence an attempt was made by the school to replenish those core values of the black subculture. One of the stated aims of the school, therefore, was to create an "extended family" atmosphere that was both nurturant and secure for the children, while instilling in them a recognition and pride in their own black heritage and tradition.

As this school was both black and low-income, its class and cultural characteristics form part of the analysis of the experience. Within this chapter I propose to discuss that which was significant and unique to the particular structure, directing my interest to the quality of the lives of the children. However, it is also important that the reader bear in mind the *different* orientation of this school; for it was actively involved in perpetuating a black cultural tradition, which, over the last two generations of urban migration, had been partially lost. It was the stated aim of this school to recapture and recreate that sense of bonded cultural community.

An interesting methodological problem arose during the analysis of my observations. I found it extremely difficult to extract patterns and theme clusters from my data. The process of extraction implies some form of separation and categorization, and there were no clearly separable themes that stood out from others: all appeared to merge. The categories that emerged upon reflection in other schools did not exist here as separate entities. For this reason I have selected as the most significant, overarching topic for this school, that which I now consider to represent a structural essence: *the merging of boundaries.*

Space, Time, and the Division of the Lived World

The separation and division of our lived-world into spatial modes and correlative activities is an underlying foundation upon which our modern Western cultural organization is based.

Consider the design of a house. There are bedrooms in which we sleep, a dining room in which we eat, a kitchen in which we cook, and a bathroom in which we perform cleansing rituals. Often a playroom in which children play and a study in which parents work complement the basic design. "My house" is frequently separated from my neighbor's by a fence, an overt boundary. Apartments, "a-partments," ensure apartness, confirm the privatization of space between myself and "the other."

However, not all social systems, nor all cultures and classes, encapsulate "my world" from "the other." In some African societies it is usual for twenty people to sleep, live, and eat within the open-faced area of a hut. Collective family and kin living is common, and in certain cases no separation rituals are observed.[1]

The experience of lived-time within our contemporary, technological culture is girded by the *demarcation* rather than the *flow* of time. Schedules, the concept of "wasted time," "time is money" orientations testify to a cost-benefit analysis of experience which is well suited to the efficient organizational network of industrial society. However, "living-in-time" is separated from "dying-in-time," from being "mentally-ill-in-time," from being "deviant-in-time." Since many institutions are created to deal with being other than "normal-in-time," our experience of the landscape of the natural world is both fragmented and confined within the boundaries of socially defined normalcy. Frequently being normal-in-time is extended to the economic and cultural domain, and those who are labeled "culturally deprived" or suffering from "sociocultural disadvantages" are often members of a low-income black culture such as we view in this chapter.

The purpose of this brief discussion has been to elucidate the culture-bound concepts of what. *is* and *is not* considered

normal-in-time. The high-boundary cultural orientation en-
demic to an industrialized technocracy needs to be situated
within its own particular social context in order to understand
what, I believe, is a distinctly different subcultural configuration—the merging of boundaries which is exemplified within
this black preschool.

The separation and division of our lived-world into strict
spatial and temporal boundaries is functional and utilitarian in
most institutional settings, of which schools are but one example. In the other centers I observed, space was demarcated
into areas for free play, motor, and cognitive activities. Time
modules were allotted to specific program events. Artifacts
and materials belonged in particular places. When the boundaries were violated, as, for example, in the Montessori School,
the boundary violation was translated into the social realm,
and *deviance* was seen to occur as a consequence.

In this preschool, however, children ride tricycles across an
area surrounded by painting easels; "hide and seek" is played
amid the artifacts of a counting lesson. Here "cognitive" space
and "physical" space merge, as do the traditional categories of
play and *work*. In a deeper vein, the merging of physical
boundaries finds its complementarity in the merging of the
cognitive and the affective, of the individual and social modes
of being. A general collective ethos emerges, and a different
childhood experience unfolds.

Space and Time—a Different Experience

During my visit this morning, I was amazed by the variety
of activities taking place simultaneously. While I sat at the
art table, two children rode bikes across the room, weaving
in among the tables. I stiffened, expecting the projects to be
knocked over, but none were. I waited for the teachers to
reprimand the children, but upon looking around I became
aware that I was the only person who considered this unusual. The bike-riding continued for a half-hour with no
staff intervention.

After breakfast I sat on the floor with Mark and Sam and
watched them building a house with blocks. While they

were building, Peter rode a bike across the room and around the block construction. The two children did not show any signs of concern as Peter continued to ride around the edifice, perilously avoiding contact.

Upon entry today, I smelled the aromas of cooked oatmeal and eggs and watched the "cook" seat four latecomers at the table for breakfast. While the children were eating, Grandma Brown sat with them, feeding the slow eaters. At another table, four adults sat cutting paper snowflakes with no children participating. Three children rolled on an adjacent mat, "play" fighting. I noticed that shoes lay strewn across the floor and that children jumped over them when moving from one area to another. Teacher Sol, the bus driver, came in, announcing a trip to the market, apparently decided on the spur of the moment. There was a sudden flurry of activity. Twenty children were ready to go, save the four latecomers. As they departed, Grandma Brown commented, "All quiet on the western front—Hail Mary!"

"Time is Not a Line But a Network of Intentionalities"[2]

Not only were spatial boundaries low—as evinced by the *integrated*, rather than *separated*, use of space, but many activities coexisted in time: a late breakfast, snowflake making, "play" fighting were all events in time which were unbounded by the rigors of a schedule. A spontaneous decision to go on an outing changed the noisy atmosphere within seconds, and a further time transformation took place. The "present" rather than "future" time orientation of the staff was conducive to that spontaneity. Events "happened" as opposed to "being planned" in advance. This modus vivendi appeared to represent a cultural configuration, reflecting, to some degree, Eliot Liebow's anthropological exploration of the present-time oriented culture of lower-class blacks in Washington.[3]

I found it interesting that four adults sat cutting out snowflakes, apparently undisturbed by the children's lack of participation in the activity. It was sufficient that the adults were engaged; there was no compulsion to engage the children at the same time. I observed this same phenomenon on many visits.

During the fall, Teacher Pat prepared a project involving leaf pasting and designs on paper. Seven of the younger children began the project but within five minutes began to lose interest. A few wandered off; one child opened the toy closet, saying, "I want to play with toys." Teacher Pat said, "O.K.," and four children began pulling out toys. Teacher Pat continued the leaf pasting, showing me her design and chatting and laughing with other adults. Three children began drawing at the table which Teacher Pat helped set up. To the left of the table, the three grandmothers were hard at work making little albums for each child.

Activities appeared to change rapidly from one form of involvement to another. There was no pressure on the children to complete an activity before beginning another, nor was there socially coercive participation. The staff were very relaxed, and each activity appeared open-ended and *directionless;* it existed for the duration of interest for its own inherent worth. The staff also participated in projects, evincing a measure of enjoyment in their own participation. It was not unusual to see adults enjoy making a project. The slow pace, the manner in which the adults "took it easy" and enjoyed their morning cup of coffee, and a daily gossip with the grandmothers created an informal, unprofessional, "unschool-like" atmosphere. This atmosphere, in turn, contributed to the simplicity and homeliness of the place. The teachers not only supervised the children's play—they also played with the children. They were physically affectionate and entertained the children so that their roles as teachers were often indistinguishable from those of parents or older brothers and sisters. One of the older female teachers, Fay, was called "Mama" by the children. My own status as participant-observer was often indistinguishable from that of the other staff members—pointing to a merging of role boundaries as I was integrated into the landscape.

I now turn to a selected citation of my personal impressions, extracted from my diary notes of the first year, as illustrative of my integration, over time, into the life of the school.

The Merging of the Participant-Observer Dichotomy

Visit 1. I can't get anything down; the kids are climbing all over me. There's too much happening. The noise level is very high but somehow doesn't bother me. Kids are very rough with each other, yet there is so much warmth and physical contact. Teachers are constantly hugging children, and the grandmothers shout instructions from their chairs in the front. They seem to command respect. The director arrives and informs me of the rules: "Kids don't walk on furniture. Teachers don't hit kids. Otherwise, no rules—we're an extension of the home." She introduced me to the staff and grandmothers, and I stood talking to the latter, feeling uncomfortable with my notebook.

Visit 6. As I enter today, I am relieved to see that all the children and staff are present and not off on a field trip. The director greets me warmly, and Teacher Ben comes up to me and asks how I am and how the work is going. Marcy and Reemie run up and climb on the table to talk to me. Reemie shows me a ring which she has made out of metal. Teacher Pat runs around the room with children riding on her back. Grandma Jones comes up to me and sneaks a packet of boiled candy from under her smock. "Here, take two or three, but don't let the kids see." As I camouflage the candy, two older children dance around me shouting, "You can't get me," in refrain and run away with my pen. I lose my notebook in the chase amid much laughter and squeals of delight as I run after them.

Visit 10. As I hang up my coat and gloves, Grandma Conrad walks up to me and shows me her arm cast. She tells me how she slipped and fell over at Christmas and broke her arm. While she is talking, Teddy runs up and says to me, "You know, I have a lot of people staying at my house but they're not all stuck together." As I smile at his vivid description, he continues, "I know some of them but not all of them." When I walk into the central area, Jack, who has become one of my favorites, runs up and hugs me shouting, "Here comes the nice lady, here she is." A few other children run up and jump onto me shouting, "Uh-huh, she's a nice lady that." I become aware of how "at home" I am and feel like a family member returning from a vacation. Teacher Pat tells me of her plans for attending school in the fall. I notice that the climbing apparatus has been moved, the tables are rearranged, and the separating doors are no longer in use.

Visit 15. Now I no longer bother to call before coming. I have become accustomed to accompanying the staff and children on spontaneous field trips: today we went to the park with Teacher Pat, and she told me the history of four-and-a-half-year-old Jack.[4] I felt very moved by her empathy and care for the child.

In this school I was unable to maintain the role of observer; from my first entry point in the fall until I left two years later at the end of the summer, I was welcomed and given a remarkable opportunity to involve myself in the life of the school. I soon learned that planned visits were inapplicable and inappropriate, that one did not make appointments, for outings would frequently be arranged on the spur of the moment. My "researcher style" changed; I took to popping in at odd times, arriving at breakfast or before lunch and staying for a few hours. I found my horizons broadened as I accompanied the different groups on trips to the railroad station, the park, the market, etc. During these outings I was afforded a unique opportunity for intimacy both with a small group of children and with one or two teachers. I learned much from casual conversations on a park bench or an occasional interlude on a bus trip.

The openness and ease with which the staff and children integrated me, a white woman, into their school was indicative, I retrospectively believe, of the familial and collective orientation of the center. The following description captures the essence of this atmosphere.

Breakfast—a familial affair. Jerry and Teacher Joe sat at the table, laughing and clowning. Teacher Joe pretended he was a paper tiger who was a magic paper eater in order to stop Jerry from eating paper and spitting it on the table. Jerry came up to me and climbed onto my lap, as oatmeal, milk, toast, and jelly were served. Grandma Brown walked up with her customary "Hi, honey" greeting and pulled me aside pointing out the new grandmother, saying, "She's a real fashion plate that; never wears the same dress twice!" While the kids waited to begin eating together,

Teacher Joe jumped up and shouted very loudly, "EAT!"
and waved his arms while the kids laughed. When Teacher
Ben came in, he hugged the children, who greeted him
while eating. Grandma Brown took Terry on her lap
and fed him the remaining portion of his breakfast, while
the children who had eaten jumped up and chased after
Teacher Joe, who was impersonating Muhammed Ali. As
the noise level rose and more children joined in the chase
after Teacher Joe, who was leaping across the equipment,
Grandma Brown shook her head saying, "That Joe, he's a
wild one that."

The merging of the different modes of the social landscape
correlated with a low-boundary consciousness of roles. Roles
were not tied to status as we observed in the hierarchical distinctions in the preceding schools but, rather, indicated cultural identity. To play-act did not demean one's "status" as a
teacher but enhanced and confirmed an essential form of
"expressiveness"—of *being* in the culture. The play-acting
and melodramatic performances were most often couched in a
language of blackness.

Play-Acting, Melodrama, and Game Playing

Cedric arrived late today, wearing a new shirt. The staff and
kids all clapped for him and made a great fuss. Teacher Pat
brought out his breakfast. Teacher Joe began to tease him
saying, "Hey, man, that's my juice," grabbing it from him
and putting it back. Teacher Joe then grabbed the toast from
Cedric's hand. "That's my toast," Cedric squealed, and all
laughed uproariously including Cedric.

Teacher Joe pretended he was a mean street thief, and the
children ran after him trying to pummel him. Teacher Joe
swaggered and fell dramatically saying, "I quit, man, you're
hitting too hard." Grandma Brown: "Spare him. Mercy.
Spare him. Spare poor ole Joe." As the children jumped on
him, he escaped to the table and lay down on top of it,
pretending he was dead. Teacher Sol then ran up and thun-
dered in mock anger, "What did you do to my friend?"
Teacher Joe then jumped up saying, "I'm going to have to

take me some boxing lessons, man. This nigger ain't doing too good today."

Saroyan climbed on top of the wooden shelving and ignored Teacher Pat's instructions to come down. Teacher Pat screwed up her face in a grimace and shouted, "If you don't get down, I'm going to hug you to death." Saroyan clambered down and ran away from Teacher Pat, who chased him around the room.

The children called each other "nigger" when taunting or teasing, as well as "brother" and "sister" when playing together. The staff used the terms in a similar way, frequently facilitating what appeared as a black consciousness of unity and togetherness.

Teacher-aide: "Sophia, I don't want no hug from you today, sister; you won't do what I say."

Cedric to Peter: "Quit that! Stop! Quit that...nigger!" (Both black, scuffling over a toy.)

The conversion of the serious to the mock heroic, the low-boundary separation between the real and the symbolic, was a recurring pattern in this school. Comedy and game playing were continuous, frequently serving to restore order and maintain balance amid the interlocking network of events.

Conflict

Much overt conflict among the children was expressed physically (pushing, punching, hairpulling, biting, hitting, etc.). In many instances the teachers would watch the children, allowing them "to fight it out," intervening only when conflict escalation presented physical danger to a child. Conflict was easily tolerated by most of the staff as "natural for kids at that age." This attitude stood in marked contrast to the "deviant" conceptions of conflict discovered at Golda Meir Nursery and at Busy Bee Montessori. Here conflict was a norm, a part of life, and was not separated out from the lived-experience, nor was the boundary between physical aggression and physical

affection marked. They were both part of the dialectical nature
of being-in-the-world. Consider Grandma Brown's statement
to a little girl:

> "Did I see you this morning? Hi there, honey. Did we have
> our fight this morning? Hmmmm? Did we have our kiss?"
> The child laughed and "play" punched and hugged her.

On a number of occasions I observed children both deal
with and resolve a conflict they were engaged in, without
adult intervention.

> During the winter, I stood near an upstairs window watch-
> ing the children play in the snow outside. I saw Dani kick
> Luke in the face. Luke fell down and cried. After a minute,
> Dani went up to Luke, put his hands on his face, and ap-
> peared to be comforting him. At that point, one of the staff
> intervened, but the child was no longer crying.

> Two children were fighting over possession of an abacus.
> Ronnie: "Hey, man, give me that." Sam: "Nooo siree! Nooo
> siree!" They continued pulling and tugging until Ronnie
> managed to grab it. Sam lifted up a chair threatening to
> throw it. There was a silence, and the two stared at each
> other for several seconds. Sam (while holding chair): "Hey,
> let's do it together." Ronnie: "Yeah, let's share it." The two
> proceeded to play together, and Teacher Pat, who had
> watched from a distance, smiled and walked off.

> Three children were throwing blocks shouting, "You
> motherfucker! Shut up!" at each other. Billy asked Cedric to
> play "bus." Cedric: "No, don't wanna do it." Billy: "Hey,
> *boy*, listen here; sit down and play bus." The three then
> began a fantasy game of "bus."

While the staff kept to a fairly consistent pattern of nonintervention in what they perceived as low-key or "normal"
conflicts, they had no hesitation in intervening forcefully and
authoritatively when this was deemed necessary—the intervention style varying with each situation.

> Jennie and Sophie were throwing blocks, narrowly missing
> each other, when Jennie was hit and began to cry. Teacher
> Pat jumped up and shouted, "That's it, that's enough." Both
> children ran off.

Two children were fighting over a toy. Seth lifted up a chair and Bennie began to scream. Teacher Fay walked over and separated the children, saying to Seth, "Come on, let's find you something else to do."

Reemie came up to Teacher Pat screaming, "Jay kicked me." Teacher Pat: "Did you tell her about it?" "No." "What did she say?" "Well, you go tell her about it."

The grandmothers frequently commented aloud about the children's behavior, intervening freely when they thought it necessary.

Benjamin lay under a table screaming. Several children stood around him trying to tease him out. Grandma Brown: "Don't you talk to him. I learned my lesson. I'll keep the rest from bothering him." A little later Teacher Fay carried Benjamin into Teacher Pat's area, saying, "I had to take Ben out of there. Not only was he in there with the truck, but then he hit someone with it." Teacher Pat: "Benjamin, that wasn't very smart." Grandma Brown: "That's that age bracket, you know. That age needs a lot of patience—a lot of patience."

The ease with which conflict was tolerated was inextricably linked to the perception of the adults that conflict is *a part of* and not *apart from* everyday life; hence, as conflict was accepted as a norm, coping styles at the center tended to be different. Explosive situations were often transformed to games, consonant with the game playing observed earlier. The following incident illustrates this rather well:

One morning Cedric and Benjamin were hitting each other, pulling hair and punching hard. They were left to "fight it out." However, when the fight escalated, Teacher Pat walked to the closet and brought out a box of beanbags. She threw one at each child and said: "Here, throw this at each other." Within minutes the children were laughing, engaged in a boisterous "beanbag fight." They were joined by other children, partitions were drawn back, and soon all thirty children, the staff, and three seventy-five-year-old grandmothers were ducking, throwing, and whooping with laughter. My notebook was downed as the fervor caught on, and I joined in the game which lasted twenty to thirty minutes, involving the whole school.

While Teacher Pat's intervention could be conceptualized as a creative resolution of the conflict through artful distraction, I understood this *game-transforming* pattern of conflict intervention as a symbol of a different mode of experiencing the world which approximates what Dahrendorf would term a "conflict model,"[5] as opposed to an "equilibrium" or "homeostatic" perspective such as we found in Golda Meir Nursery and the Montessori Center. Conflict is not viewed as systemically unhealthy, nor is it dysfunctional, for within this model the social system is experienced as a continually contested power struggle between opposing groups with clashing interests. The low-income black world is clearly divergent from the dominant white middle-class milieu. Living for a low-income black person is a series of conflicts, and this reality is embodied in the lifestyle and cultural modalities transmitted from one generation to another.[6] What we have observed here might be an example of this cultural transmission, for at Martin Luther King Center, the free expression of conflict was consonant with the lifeworld and lifestyle of lower-class black culture. However, it appeared that a conflict norm also allowed for bonding and empathy on the part of the children, which was unusual in the other centers I had observed. The pattern of conflict discovered here was dialectical, with aggression and cooperative empathy interwoven into the social fabric.

Given that this school resembled a conflict model in its characteristics, that it was relatively unstructured, often bordering on the anarchic, where did the stability, the network of consistent norms come from?

The Grandmothers: Bearers of Tradition and Links with the Past

The grandmothers, in particular Grandma Brown, generated a powerful presence in the classroom. From their matriarchal seats in the front of the room, each would act as nurturer, comforter, and disciplinarian. Invariably it was their word that carried the most weight. They were indulgent, yet extremely authoritarian toward the children, and appeared to derive tremendous enjoyment from their foster role. They even made little gifts for the children (books, albums, etc.), knitted them articles of clothing, and took great pride in the children's "cute" sayings and achievements. I frequently heard the three of them talking among themselves about the children and laughing at their antics. They were also very caring and affectionate toward the children.

> Grandma Jones noticed that Tan was sitting alone at the breakfast table with an unfinished bowl of cereal. She went to the child, commenting, "Don't like seeing a little one sitting there all alone," and sat down, put the child on her lap, and proceeded to feed her.

> India ran across the room crying because Teacher Pat had not read her the book she wanted. She ran up to Grandma Conrad, who promptly seated her on her lap saying, "Well, yes, I'll read it to you, sweetheart," and dried the child's tears.

When the children became "tiresome," the grandmothers adopted a no-nonsense attitude, and often became quite rejecting.

> Grandma Brown shouted at Benjamin to "leave that truck alone." Benjamin obeyed and approached Grandma. She retorted, "Stay away from me; I had enough of you today. I don't want to know you." Ben walked away with his head down and approached Teacher Pat saying, "I won't do that anymore. I won't hurt anyone anymore with it." Teacher Pat: "You won't? O.K. I'll get it for you." Grandma Brown turned to me and said, "I knew when he came this morning, he'd be evil. I knew his attitude."

> During breakfast, Grandma Brown sat next to little Dion (two-and-a-half years), and he kicked her. She retorted, "I'll kick you back. My foot's bigger than yours," and then turned to me and winked. "Dion won't talk to me anymore because I don't have my wig no more. He doesn't know me."

The warmth and love meted out by Grandma Brown were extremely powerful, and she herself was a compelling woman.

Withdrawal of her love was a powerful deterrent to "evil" behavior on the part of the children. A pattern of "straight" talking was characteristic of all three matriarchs:

> During breakfast Grandma Conrad was feeding Jack banana bread and cereal and ignoring Sam, who had annoyed her earlier. Sam, after unsuccessfully attempting to capture her attention, said, "Shut up." Grandma Conrad: "You don't say 'shut up' to me. That's very bad. If you're angry at me, you can swear at me, but don't say 'shut up!'" Sam bowed his head.

The children never, to my knowledge, disobeyed the grandmothers. They would defy the staff on occasion, but not the grandmothers. The staff were extremely respectful toward the grandmothers and would often turn to them for the final word or command.

> Lester threw his blocks on the floor as his group was about to leave for the market. Teacher Pat grimaced and Grandma Brown shouted, "That wasn't very smart. Now, you pick them up, otherwise, no market." Lester did as he was told, and the group departed amid much confusion and noise. Grandma Brown: "We've got to organize better than that. It's working in the blind."

The grandmothers appeared to represent the vital link between "home/family" and "school." They were the bearers of a traditional black culture[7] which now reemerged in the context of Martin Luther King preschool. They helped replicate and transmit those social bonds which, historically, anchored the black family of the South.[8] The interactions at this center took place in the shadow of the grandmothers' presence.

A Traditional Authoritarian Discipline

The staff displayed an easy familiarity of both speech and action when interacting with the children. There was no "preschool jargon," no sophisticated verbalization of action, as in the first two schools of the study. While there was no articulated ideology about a "free/open" classroom, this school provided a free, spontaneous environment for the children, based on a traditional, authoritarian foundation. The limits were clear and unambiguous and consonant with the children's own cultural background. I did not observe any particular preplanned mode of discipline; each individual staff member appeared to intervene naturally and deal with the children as the situation arose. There was no discipline "problem," for when the staff gave commands, they were most often obeyed. When they were not, the staff would shout, become more forceful or punitive, and order would be restored.

The younger staff members—Teachers Pat, Joe, and Sol—resembled older brothers or sisters, as opposed to Teacher Fay, who was called "Mama." Hence, a network of family members were in evidence at the center, and one observed a pattern of "family" discipline with different styles among the "family" members.

> During group time, Sarah kicked Terry. Teacher Fay (sternly): "Don't you do that; say 'sorry.'" Terry kicked Sarah back. Teacher Fay: "No, that's not right either, stop it." They both obeyed.

> Dani kicked David during singing. Teacher Pat (in a mock angry tone): "Don't kick my friend, David. Nooo! Would you like him to kick you? Nooo! Come here." She picked up Dani and "play" punched him. She later told me that he reminded her of her younger brother.

> During a singing rehearsal for "parents' night," Benny and Sam were hitting and punching each other. Teacher Fay shouted at them to "stop hitting! Ain't nothing to do but listen." Later, after the rehearsal, Teacher Joe decided to take them on an outing as a surprise. "O.K., you were real good today. Let's go get your coats."

The director, Mrs. Tally, herself a mother of seven, espoused what she called "a traditional discipline of firmness and love," which was complemented by her professional training as an early childhood educator. Consider the following incident with Larry, perceived to be a "difficult" child.

> Teacher Sol brought in Larry from outside, telling Mrs. Tally that he had been "throwing rocks and biting kids." Mrs. Tally told Larry he had to stay inside for ten minutes until he calmed down. Larry screamed, cried, kicked, tore

up an empty box of kleenex, kicked the sliding book cases, and threw over a chair. Teacher Pat mildly remonstrated with him, smiling, and winked at me. Mrs. Tally picked him up and held him on her lap while he kicked and screamed. After ten minutes of screaming he quieted down, and Mrs. Tally kissed him, asking Grandmother Conrad to "bring a puzzle over for me and Larry to do together," and kissed him again. Larry began playing with the puzzle and was joined by two other children. Mrs. Tally walked off and later told me how much better Larry was; that he had another brother at X (a state correctional house) and had a fear of falling asleep because when he wakes up, there is no one at his house; that Teacher Sol sometimes drove to five different houses when taking him home, looking for someone to leave him with, as his mother was often not there.

The care and affection that Mrs. Tally expressed to Larry, the "casual" way in which the other staff and children handled his violent tantrum, was impressive. I became aware of the value of the center, of the core "home" function it served for so many children, and the relative lack of labeling that occurred here. There was a far higher tolerance of deviance; or, perhaps, the *boundaries between deviance and normalcy were low;* there was no stark dichotomy but, rather, a *merging* of social categories; hence Larry's behavior was no threat to the social order. Since Larry's family context was not unusual within this setting, his behavior was not considered extraordinary either. Teacher Pat smiled, almost amused during his fit of rage, an attitude which contributed to the atmosphere of tolerance and openness. Larry was not "maladjusted," "semi-retarded," or in need of "therapy"; rather, he was a "tough one," "a naughty kid" who was said to need firm but loving handling. Here he was not isolated by the community, not sent to a correctional institution like his brother, but rather integrated into the landscape; a landscape with sufficiently low boundaries between "normalcy" and "deviancy" that he was not excluded from the life of the school, or scapegoated. In the other schools, no doubt his behavior would have been construed as deviant. Hence we realize the inherent social and cultural relativity of these labels. Larry was a part of a conflict-oriented culture; to express his inner conflict and rage was thus acceptable within this milieu.

While the social perceptions of the staff at this school clearly differed from the mainstream thinking on early childhood, the center was, nevertheless, a social system with its own organizational structure and sets of sanctions and patterns of "acceptable" behavior. Because its norms differed from those of other, "white," preschool institutions, its process of early institutionalization took a different route—a route that was largely anti-institutional vis-à-vis the macrosocial system and hence discontinuous with the patterns of corporate education. Yet the school performed a strong socialization function that was continuous with lower-class black culture and black identity. The anti-norms in this setting were clearly behaviors that threatened the cultural tradition. One of the strong negative sanctions that I observed here dealt with rugged individualism and anticollective behavior.

The Socialization of a Collective Ethos

Three children were playing with a doll set and began to squabble over possession of the doll. Teacher Pat immediately intervened, "You can't play with it because you don't know how to share it," and took it away.

Teacher Pat was working with Nellie at the table doing object classification. Nellie did not want to share the objects with the other children nor take turns with Teacher Pat. She began to cry. Teacher Pat shouted, "Quit it," and picked her up screaming and left her in the hallway. When she continued to scream, Teacher Pat picked up a toy and threw it to her to play with. As Nellie continued to scream and cry, Teacher Pat muttered, "Little brat," and shouted, "I'm going to take you to the bathroom in a minute." One of the other aides picked her up and tried to soothe her, but she continued to cry softly. Teacher Pat continued to work with the other children. Nellie then climbed onto Grandma Jones's lap, and Grandma Jones whispered to her to "Go say sorry to Pat." Teacher Pat looked up and said, "Are you feeling better now?" No answer. "Why don't you come over here by me. I don't like you when you're hollering for no good reason, acting like that. Why don't you come back over here by me?" Nellie went to Teacher Pat, who cuddled her and lifted her onto her lap.

Teacher Pat's initial harsh treatment of Nellie followed by an affectionate "making up" was typical of the sanctions and punitive attitudes on the part of the staff, which invariably dealt with nonsharing acts. It was not considered desirable or legitimate to be possessive or fiercely individualistic. Sharing and playing together were strongly encouraged, and children tended to play cooperatively and in groups.

This morning I watched three children playing together building a train out of dominoes. In the adjacent area, five children transformed a swing into a bed. I looked around the room and noticed that all the children were playing in groups. I did not observe any individual play.

Teacher Fay brought in a new "toy" today—pegboards with pegs ostensibly designed for individual designs. I watched Billy and Sarah and Nellie turn one pegboard over and stick the pegs into it, thereby making a raft; they then took it to the water table together and took turns playing with it.

The creativity and flexibility of the children was interesting. They transformed the materials to their own imaginative uses. Dominoes became a train; a swing became a hammock; a pegboard became a raft. In all these instances the play transformations took place collectively, not individually.

During wintertime, a field trip was announced in the morning. Mrs. Tally took out a large box containing mittens and boots; the children took these from the box, put on their coats, and ran outside. I did not observe any squabbles of "mine" or "yours" over the clothes.

It was the first day of spring, and children were told they could play outside. Everyone, including the staff and director, rushed downstairs and began carrying out the heavy play equipment together.

The collective sharing and spirit of unity and cooperation were striking features of the school. The language of the staff-child interactions reinforced this collective orientation.

The staff often spoke to the children in a way that emphasized their commonality rather than their differences, employing a language of analogue rather than comparison.

"I have shoes like yours," or "What do we have the same

today?" or (to Larry) "I know the same people at *X* where your brother is."

This language of analogue contrasted markedly with the typical preschool focus on differences observed in other centers. One did not hear questions such as "Who has new shoes on today?"—questions that separate the "old shoe wearers" from the "new shoe wearers" and thus emphasize possessiveness. Rather, the focus was on, what do we have in common? This orientation, consonant with the merging of boundaries theme, facilitated a pervasive collective ethos.

A Retrospective Note on a Personal Learning Experience

During the winter of my first year at this school, I set up interview times with several regular staff members on a Wednesday afternoon when most children took naps. I arrived at 1:00 P.M., planning to spend the next three hours interviewing individual staff members in an open-ended fashion in the community center board room. I was therefore somewhat taken aback to find five staff members, including the director, all waiting for me in the board room, having arranged for aides to watch the children who were not napping. My initial reaction was one of being thrown off balance, wondering, "How can I handle five staff members all together? Will they be honest? Won't they be intimidated by the director, etc.?" I soon realized, however, that I was imposing my perception upon a different reality. The director informed me, "We like having our discussions together; we learn more that way—and don't worry, we have plenty of different ideas." As I sat down in the board room I was struck by the significance of this experience. The hierarchy distinctions were blurred—teachers talked freely as did the director and I became aware of the *collective structure* of the interview. Whereas I had attempted an individualized experience by setting up separate times for each interview, they, "my subjects," had decided that was an undesirable medium of expression. As Teacher Pat put it: "We like to argue with each other and with May (the director)." I realized that, had I arrived armed with a traditional interview instrument, I would have learned almost

nothing; that my initial reservations had emerged from my
own individualistic and narrow mind-set, believing that
even open-ended interviews are best conducted separately.
I learned much from that experience, which I retrospectively believe was an integral part of the collective
ethos and merging of boundaries theme that pervaded the
school landscape.

During the interview, my previous conversation with
Teacher Sol, and later discussions, I realized that for the first
time I had observed a center where what the staff *told* me and
what they actually *did* somehow matched—where theory and
action came together in a rather unusual way.

Teacher Pat: "I'd rather be a bigger sister than a 'Miss Mc-
Crae' teacher. I love kids—they crack me up. I became
interested in it [daycare] through my little brother."

Director (May Tally): "In the average black family, the
child is taught to share. We encourage that here. We try and
encourage a family atmosphere. Credentials aren't as important as staff who love children."

Teacher Fay (herself the mother of eight children and instrumental in setting up the center four years previously):
"We don't keep records and we don't label kids. We see
ourselves as an extended family. We never force them to get
into activities. I feel like I have a second home here."

Teacher Sol: "I'm aware of the social background of these
kids—what they face in everyday living. We try and make
their experiences meaningful. We foster sharing and kindness. The kids are really into being kind to each other—in
tune with other kids' feelings."

While thinking critically about the surprising continuity
between the stated philosophical intent of the staff and the
landscape that was created for the children, I perceived that
ideological discontinuity did not lie *within* this preschool,
which was a cohesive microsocial system, but in the relation of
the preschool to the larger society. While black awareness,
black cultural identity, and values of cooperation rather than
competition were entirely consistent with the subculture, they
did not serve the interests of corporate schooling in general.

Much criticism was leveled against this school by university

educators and external educational sources. Funding was precarious, and the "cognitive curriculum" was considered by the
outside world to be poor.

The attitude of the staff toward learning fluctuated from
laissez-faire to a stringent "back to the basics" orientation.
The director was concerned by the criticism; the grandmothers wanted the kids to "learn to read and write like other,
white kids." Hence, when the kids were taught, the method
and style of teaching tended to be traditional, with a heavy
reliance on drill and rote learning; the content of what was
being taught was most often developmentally inappropriate.
The staff appeared caught in a sea of in-betweenness; they
were ambivalent, often indifferent, and unwilling to subject
themselves or the children to a rigorous curriculum. There was
an inconsistent imposition of a very traditional learning environment upon the children, which, while not taken seriously
or strongly enforced by all staff members, tended to create a
confusion of expectations at the center.

Although the cognitive curriculum was not a high priority in
this school, there was a concern about the lack of cognitive
skills of the children, who, by conventional standards, compared unfavorably with their peers in other centers. If one
evaluated these children according to current psychological
diagnostic criteria, many, no doubt, would be labeled "slow
learners" or "socioculturally retarded." Their vocabulary was
not as extensive as their average white, middle-income
counterparts; their discrimination and classification skills
were not at the "correct" preoperational level; they did not sit
still and concentrate for long periods of time (a condition
sometimes known as "hyperactivity" in current school
management jargon). Yet they were socially cooperative and
affectionate; they were curious and bright; they asked in-
telligent questions; they were active and independent. Above
all, they were free to *play*.

One therefore should question whether there was something "wrong" with these children, or, rather, whether there is
something alarmingly unbalanced about current applied developmental theory, whose inferences about children's
psychological processes are often based on a deficient pedagogic awareness of cultural differences. This deficiency, in

turn, biases the orientation of the early childhood field in general, and a fundamental perspective is lost—the world of play of the child.

I was impressed by the manner in which the children of Martin Luther King Childcare Center were permitted to experience a childhood relatively unfettered by institutional constraints. Through their freedom to play, they transformed their landscape of space and time as the boundaries between "school" and "family" merged in the informal and spontaneous life at the center. That merging, in turn, gave many children a sense of being "at home" in the world.

8

Pine Woods Free School

Pine Woods is a private, nonprofit "free school" which includes a preschool, a kindergarten, and an elementary school. It is located on a large, secluded property surrounded by overhanging trees and a vast grassy play area. The buildings on the property are old and a little run-down, but the country-like atmosphere is pleasant and refreshing.

The school is modeled on the educational philosophy of A. S. Neill's *Summerhill* and is one of the few "alternative" free schools in the area.

The preschool, the subject of the following study, offers a morning nursery program which extends into afternoon daycare. The morning session has approximately fifteen children and in the afternoon the number increases to about twenty. Fees are on a sliding scale. Scholarships are offered for those who cannot afford the tuition. While the majority of children are drawn from middle-income families, a sizable number come from A.D.C. and low-income homes. The school is fairly well integrated, and parental involvement is strong. Parents serve on educational and planning committees; some work there as volunteers; others assist in maintenance, fundraising, and other such tasks. There are shared social events, potlucks, and outings. Because the school operates on a shoe-string budget, finances are a constant headache for the director.

The preschool is a self-contained unit with five rooms including a bathroom and kitchen. The children move freely from one interfacing room to another, and there is only one interior door, which closes off the little dress-up room. The snack room contains long tables and is also used for arts and crafts. Apart from that, the functions of the other rooms change from month to month.

Ideology and the "Unstructured Structure"

The function of the child is to live his own life—not
the life that his anxious parents think he should live,
nor a life according to the purpose of the educator
who thinks he knows what is best. All this interference and guidance on the part of adults only produces a generation of robots.[1]

At this center there was no formal organizational structure,
there was no planned curriculum, no division of the day into
time blocks. Children were encouraged to choose freely whatever activity they wished to engage in. The only structured
activities occurred around eating and sleeping rituals, which
took place at appropriately designated times.

The activity choices ranged from drawing, building, cutting,
storytelling, and reading to project-making. If a child wished
to participate in any of the above, he would ask one of the
adults for assistance in setting up the activity. However, most
children appeared to opt for "free play." They played in
groups of two or three for long periods of time without adult
intervention.

The model for Pine Woods, Summerhill School, was founded
in 1921 in England, by A. S. Neill. Its main tenets are:
a belief in the child's own natural ability to grow and develop
in relative freedom from adult interference; a belief in the
child's inherent curiosity and desire to learn; a belief that
learning occurs through *doing;* and a belief that social and
emotional growth is more important than intellectual growth.

The ideological commitment to freedom for the child, the
opposition to any formal curriculum, any demarcation of time
and space, are the most compelling structural characteristics of
Pine Woods, in whose handbook we read:

> Children mingle with others as they will. A class occurs
> whenever two or more people decide to explore the same
> area of interest. A child is free to go on his or her own, to be
> with other children, or to work with a staff member. Time is
> scheduled according to the individual child's (or group of
> children's) pursuit.

In this center, the ideological commitment to the existential
freedom of the child undergirds the educational program and
the subsequent interaction patterns and relationships.

There is a firm advocacy of the belief that the primary world for the child is the social and interpersonal. The acquisition of future-oriented cognitive skills is considered secondary to an active involvement in the life of the school. Gay, the head teacher of the preschool, remarked to me:

> They need love and kindness. Those are the things that they must have as little kids—learn how to get along with each other and how to deal with each other. Skills and subject areas they'll pick up later when they need it. They only learn new things by doing.

As the staff tended to encourage a play rather than work orientation on the part of the children, much of the day was spent in interactive free play. These unstructured patterns of play generated a fascinating structure of their own.

> Kelly and I were playing on the floor with blocks. Kelly was a new arrival to the school, having previously attended Busy Bee Montessori Center. The following conversation took place between us. Kelly: "Did I come here when I was three years old?" Val: "I don't know, what do you think?" Kelly: "No, I didn't. I used to go to a school where there was an Indian lady." Val: "And what did you do there?" Kelly: "There were no toys, so we never had clean-up time, but we did lessons at the school and counting." Val: "And what else did you do?" Kelly: "And we did lessons and we did work." Val: "And what do you do here?" Kelly: "Here, I play with other kids—and I play." Val: "Did you play at the other school too?" Kelly: "No, we did work and lessons—and we put away work."

This child readily discriminated between "play" and "work" at the two centers under discussion. Whereas at Golda Meir, Busy Bee Montessori, and Lollipop Learning Center, the children were required to *work* and allowed limited "free play" time, here no distinction was made between activity, involvement, and interactive play. We also note how the idea of play-as-fun and work-as-antifun emerges at an extremely young age. In this school, play was ongoing and uninterrupted. It was thus a conducive atmosphere to explore the play life of children in a group setting.

There is a constant flow of movement through the rooms. Children spontaneously move from place to place. Some look aimless, some seem bored, others are excited and "hard at play." Joanie announced that there would be a movie, and three children ran up and joined her. They switched off the lights in the block room, donned old clothes for costumes, and made "play-play" curtains. The four children built a stage out of the large blocks and began jumping off it, pretending to be monsters and other "scary things." As the noise level increased to a din, Teacher Jean walked out, closing the sliding doors and said, "I'm going to leave; it hurts my ears." I stayed in to watch and experienced the noise level as almost unbearable, but noticed that none of the four children appeared bothered by the noise.

This morning I watched the block room change into a jungle as three girls formed a "hunting gang." Paula: I'm going hunting, O.K.?" Jenny: "O.K., bye." Diane to Paula (who was carrying back a block): "Is that big meat you killed?" Paula nods. Jenny (climbing down): "I'm taking my gun." Paula: "I'll hold your hand in case you're frightened." Jenny: "No, I'm not frightened. I'm rough!"

The imagination and creative fantasy play of these children was multifaceted, and the nonstereotypical role-playing of the girls was striking. No artifact occupied a stable position in the environment, and the children were *free to create their own landscape.* Anything they had could become what they wanted it to be. The block room could be transformed into a movie theater one day, a jungle the next. A block could serve as a gun, an animal, or a movie projector. The blocks could be steps or they could all be moved out of the block room and become refrigerator items to be packed into a toy chest. The multiple functions of objects were part of the transforming nature of play in this environment, which bore the imprint of active children.

I was playing with Sandi today, and she pretended she was cooking a meal. Sandi offered me "food" on a plate with a spoon. Remembering a similar incident at Golda Meir Nursery School, I tried to replicate my reactions, and I licked the plate. The little girls replied, "You eat like a doggie." A few seconds later, I pulled a face and said, "Ugh, I think it needs more sugar." Sandi ran to the table and brought a block saying, "Here, here's the sugar. Shake it and pour it."

This experience differed markedly from a similar one at Golda Meir Nursery the previous month. There Myron was engaged in elaborately setting a table with plates and cutlery. He handed me a saucer with a fork, saying, "Taste it. See if you like it." I licked the saucer and he said, "No, with a fork." I used the fork, pulled a face, and said, "Ugh, needs a bit more sugar." Myron stood looking at me, seemingly perplexed and floored by the unexpected demand. I retracted by saying, "Oh, that's O.K. I can do without," and proceeded to "eat it up."

The facility and ease with which Sandi handled a new demand which was external to her immediate fantasy structure was markedly different from that of Myron's seeming perplexity. I wondered whether Sandi's flexibility and spontaneity, as opposed to Myron's reaction of bewilderment, was related to the rigidity or freedom of the respective environments and the extent to which children were permitted to endow their landscape with significance and to experience their own activity as transforming the world.

Teacher Gay and Play

During the period of my involvement with Pine Woods, I became aware of how my experiences at this center were mediated by the powerful presence of the head teacher. I had visited the school prior to Teacher Gay's time, and it had been significantly different—more chaotic, more laissez-faire. However, with Gay's entry I saw the "free school" philosophy merge with the remarkable teaching abilities of an unusual woman. Gay, a mother of five children, the youngest of whom attended the center with her, was a southern black woman who had "made it" out of poverty and through college; and she brought a unique cultural and individual influence to this preschool. In analyzing what I had discovered here, I became aware of how much Gay's presence and personality positively influenced this preschool.

Teacher Gay could spontaneously defuse difficult, chaotic, or tedious situations and transform them into games. She frequently participated with the children when they were playing fantasy games, and embodied cognitive learning within the framework of game playing.

During snack time Ray started stamping on the floor with his feet and kicking his neighbors. Other children followed his example and began stamping on the floor until the room was in an uproar. Teacher Gay walked in and shouted, "Simon says stamp your feet," and the children stamped louder, laughing. Teacher Gay then shouted, "Simon says, clap your hands. Simon says snap your fingers. Simon says touch your nose," etc., until the noise subsided, and the children were involved in the group game and then ate their snack.

When Teacher Gay served water and graham crackers today, one child asked, "Why do we have water today?" Teacher Gay: "Because all that sweet stuff isn't good for you." Marty: "But why do we need water?" Teacher Gay: "Why do plants need water?" Chorus of children: "To grow." A discussion about growing, babies, and ages followed. Teacher Gay picked up on the theme of ages and spontaneously devised a group game around addition and subtraction through finger play. When Les asked for another cracker, Teacher Gay replied, "You'll have to pretend because it's one hour until lunchtime," and pretended to eat an invisible cracker. The child imitated her and laughed.

Teacher Gay sat on the floor with three children playing "This Little Piggie Went to Market." As she played, she engaged the children in counting activities and storytelling. She sat with the children on her lap, alternately cuddling and kissing them. Later when the children were gathered around the table for snacks, she called the register in the following fashion, "Is Kari here?" and all the children would look around and point to the child and all would chorus, "Yes." When she called, "Is Jason here?" and the children chorused, "No," she explained that he was sick and could not come.

Teacher Gay was very warm and motherly to the children. All the children appeared to gravitate toward her, and there was a great deal of mutual physical affection. Her calling of the register was but one instance of the manner in which she "personalized" the room. Each child's presence or absence was felt by all.

During lunchtime two children crawled under the table and laughed. Teacher Gay laughed too, and shouted, "O.K., I'm going to get your lunch and eat it all up." The children scrambled out from under the table and began to eat their lunch.

Teacher Gay described herself to me as more "a mother than a teacher" in this school. When I complimented her on her skillful handling of the potential lunchroom chaos, she replied laughingly, "Oh, I grew up with a lot of humor too." Teacher Gay's style was unique. It differed markedly from the intervention styles of the other staff members, particularly in relation to conflict.

Ideology and Conflict

In this school there was an articulated ideology of conflict expression. Children were encouraged to air their feelings of anger and permitted to express both verbal and physical aggression toward each other. The staff attempted to facilitate conflict resolution on the part of the children, independent of teacher intervention.

> Vera threatened Jody with a stick and Jody cried. Jody then went to tell Teacher Jean that Vera had been unfair to her. Teacher Jean, "That's Vera's business," and to Jody (still crying): "Jody, if you have a problem, you settle it."

> Two children were preparing snacks together with Teacher Jean. Karen walked in and pushed Kelly, who spilled the milk. Kelly: "Stop it, Karen, you made me spill." Karen to Teacher Jean: "She won't let me do it." Teacher Jean: "Well, they started doing it, and it's up to them if they want anyone to help."

On a number of occasions I observed children taking the initiative in peer intervention without the prompting of a teacher.

> During group play, Casey hit Fay. Fay began to cry. Terry turned to Casey and said angrily, "Don't hurt her." Rachel, another member of the group, said, "Casey, you shouldn't have hit her with the block." At that point, Teacher Gay intervened and rebuked Casey.

Andy and Lennie constructed a slide out of boards in the block room. Several other children joined them when they saw the slide. Andy began throwing wooden blocks down the slide which bounced off the edges. Lennie: "Andy, I told you not to do that! You could hurt someone." Andy: "O.K., then, I'll go to my bed and smoke a joint." He pretended to be smoking while lying on the floor. Lenny: "Don't smoke in bed; it'll burn up." Andy: "Hey, man, I'm getting out of here," and leaves.

While certain children often took the initiative in peer intervention and displayed a strong sense of responsibility and sensitivity to others, such behavior was not widespread. The most frequent conflict incidents were bullying and intimidation of children *and* staff—the "survival of the fittest" appeared to be the norm. In this manner Pine Woods, while articulating a rationalized commitment to conflict, differed markedly from Martin Luther King Center, where conflict was "natural," and did not present the ensuing problem we view here.

Melanie was playing on the swing outside when Ray came up, pushed her off, and took the swing. Melanie did not resist nor cry, but wandered off.

During movie time, Michael went up to Steve and pushed him very hard so that he fell over his chair and began to cry. As the other teachers and children looked on in silence, Teacher Gay walked up, held Michael, and said, "Is there any other way you could do that? Would you like to be pushed off a chair like that?" Michael: "Well, it's my chair." Teacher Gay: "Well, could you ask him? Let's find another chair."

Kathy walked by Ray proudly carrying a crown that she had just made at the project table. Ray pulled it away and Kathy cried. Ray then broke it and stamped on it and Kathy started screaming. Ray picked up his shoes from the floor and threw them at her. Teacher Jean: "Don't throw shoes; seriously, you can hurt someone. You can play, but you don't throw shoes." A volunteer held the little girl and comforted her while Teacher Jean took Ray into the kitchen saying, "Come here. I want to talk to you."

During snack time, Michael called Sally "a bit fat fucker," and hit her on the head. Sally looked at Teacher Beth and said, "He's hitting me." Teacher Beth did not respond and Michael ran off.

The refusal or inability of the staff to deal with Ray, the aggressor, or with Michael, resulted in a paradoxical situation. The teachers were ideologically committed to the *expression* rather than the *repression* of aggression, yet their attitude of nonintervention in the above cited examples led to a denial of both Ray's and Michael's acts, both of which were clearly hurtful to other children. By pointedly ignoring the intentionally hurtful nature of these children's acts, the staff were in fact denying both children's aggression. In the crown incident, the teacher chose to focus on the shoe throwing, not on the destruction of Kathy's carefully made crown.

While Teacher Gay usually intervened by encouraging a child to understand the other's feelings, the rest of the staff members tended to assume a stance of *nonaction*. Many of these adults, in fact, appeared to be intimidated by the ideology that they espoused, i.e., the need to be nonauthoritarian. Though they displayed tremendous respect for the children, they would frequently subject themselves to insults from these same children.

Ellie ran up behind Teacher Beth and hit her hard on the back, shouting, "You fucker," at her. Teacher Beth (very quietly): "Hey, that hurts. I know you're angry, but that hurts." Ellie hit her again, but she did not respond, and Ellie ran off and began to suck her thumb. Soon afterward, she walked up behind Jody and pushed her off her chair. Jody cried, and Teacher Beth looked on but did not intervene. Jody soon stopped crying and Ellie walked off.

A new staff member walked in today, and three children immediately ran up and began taunting him with "Hey, you fucker; hey, you fucker." He did not respond and no staff intervened.

A great deal of the children's aggression appeared to be directed toward testing the limits of the respective staff members. How far did a child have to go, I often wondered, in

order for staff members to express direct anger, thereby over-
coming their own powerful ideological restraints. In many instances, the inter-child aggression appeared to result from a
lack of response on the part of the staff to a blatant act of
aggression against the staff themselves.

Sensitive as they were to the needs and rights of the children, the teachers displayed a paradoxical and demeaning attitude to themselves. I wondered how many of the adults in
that school would tolerate from other adults the treatment they
sometimes received from the children.

Now it was the adults who were oppressed by their very
commitment to an ideology of unlimited freedom for the child.
This ideology often rendered them powerless and unable to
respond appropriately to the children. Such inaction paradoxically led to a situation where many children displayed not
cooperative, but *competitive* behavior, not social but *anti-
social* behavior, frequently testing adult limits of tolerance
and endurance. The staff either denied their own anger or
tried to verbalize it rationally; but the children did not follow
their example. The toughest and strongest in the environment
became bullies, and the norms of individualism and self-
interest flourished in an atmosphere that was dedicated,
ideologically, to social cooperation.

Thus, in this "free school" we see the dialectical struggle
between freedom and authority played out in a countercultural, early childhood institution which became the testing
ground for a particular idea of childhood—a childhood of play,
of freedom of expression, of respect for children's rights. On
the other hand, this often resulted in the abdication of the role
and responsibility of the teacher.

In this way, I believe, the school went overboard, tilting the
precarious balance between an authoritarian and a laissez-
faire environment. A double standard arose: expectations for
the adults were very different from those that operated for the
children. Children were placed in the position of not assuming responsibility for their actions, for they were protected by
an overarching ideology that favored their rights "to be" and
"to do," which fostered individualistic behavior and made it
difficult for the children to develop a sense of reciprocity.

The clash between ideology and culture was acutely evident here; for while the school itself was a countercultural institution, paradoxically it reflected the dominant trends in the social system against which it was struggling— competition, laissez-faire individualism, and a "survival of the fittest" ethos.

To the extent that they had succeeded in creating a counter-culture of respect and cooperation within their landscape, the adults were true to their own ideology; but this did not easily permeate the child society, because the staff did not commit themselves to the pedagogical task of *teaching* the children.[2] The children, too, needed the experience of being-with-others-in-the-world in as authentic a manner as possible. But lacking limits and, on the part of most teachers, active encouragement to behave in socially cooperative ways, the children were thrown into ambiguity.

In this way the leveling of obstacles and the abdication of the role of the teacher rather, in Bergmann's words, "simply gives way to the pecking order of the crudest . . . it means that those who think that mere withdrawal creates free-dom for the children in their care are simply wrong—this self-indulgent recipe produces nearly the opposite effect. But it also means that in this version the possibility of a genuine 'free school' has not yet been tried, and that it, therefore, has not begun to be refuted."[3]

3

9

The Erosion of Childhood

Childhood as a life-phase is becoming at home in
the world.
> *Donald Vandenberg*
> BEING AND EDUCATION[1]

Does a social space for childhood still exist in our modern
technological era—a space where the child can become *at
home* in the world, where she can also be the subject, not only
the object, of history? By examining specific forms of a modern
childhood through an interpretative ethnography of child life
within these institutional contexts, I return once again to the
question posed at the opening of this book: is childhood a
natural state or a social invention?

We cannot deny the "historicity of childhood" any more
than we can deny our own human historicity. Childhood *is* a
natural state, a life phase of the human project, but the particular *forms* of childhood created through the social ideology of
"schooling" embedded in early childhood institutions have, in
many ways, eroded that life phase and imposed a false structure of meaning on the ontological development of the child.

Play as Constitutive of the Being of the Child

The lived-world of the child, the mode of being-
in-the-world that is characteristic of childhood, is
such that the child lives in a world that invites exploration. He exists within purified reflection
wherein the pre-reflective realm is clear of the

subterfuges and bad faith of the realm of reflection.
He is consequently, authentically, there in the
world. He lives directly into the world, prior to the
development of the subject-object split, prior to the
alienation from the immediate world. The child's
open communion with the world in his play, in fact,
is not merely the place wherein the individual's
relationship to being is formed, it is the primordial
and originary relation to being.[2]

The child lives in open communion with the world, and the
world, in turn, invites exploration from the child. Things in
the world challenge the child, disclose themselves to the
child; and the child as *Dasein* is intentionally directed upon
the beckoning world.[3]

Play is the mode through which the child realizes herself. It
is through play that the child restructures, invents, makes
history and transforms her given *en-soi* reality;[4] for the transforming nature of play allows the child to become fully realized as a human being.[5] It is vital that the child be permitted
to live this life phase fully, to play and let "the things themselves" disclose themselves in their original glory; for things
in the beckoning world *are* what they appear to be to the child.
Hence the child, "green and golden" as "huntsman and
herdsman" and as "prince of the apple towns" makes his history "about the lilting house" and transforms the structures of
the life-world. Herein lies the history-making power of the
child, the mode through which the child existentially imprints
her mark upon the landscape and changes it.

While meaningful labor has been viewed as the primary
mode essential for the development of the being of the adult,
so too, play should be seen as the primary mode for the child
who is involved in becoming. *The child becomes herself
through play.*

But play, as the child's praxis upon the world, should not
be dichotomized from work; for the playing child is a working
child—engaged in meaningful, purposive activity. This
work-play dialectic is a fundamental theme of childhood
which is unrecognized and denied in most schools. The separation that the adult world imposes between "work" and
play and the demarcation of these activities into specific

contexts is not part of the structure of childhood. Work, in the adult world, is defined by particular spatial and temporal boundaries and linked to the productive functions of the marketplace in a capitalist technocracy (and no doubt in a socialist technocracy as well!). Play, too, takes place in specific spatial and temporal frames and is highly organized and hierarchically structured so that "recreation" and "leisure" time have themselves become sciences and industries with corresponding experts in the technology of play.

But children do not view the world like that, at least not until they are taught to do so. They are in the world; they act upon the world; they discover things in the world; and in so doing and acting, they are fulfilling a fundamental human activity of intentionality and purposiveness. Consider the example of the intense investigation by a fifteen-month-old baby of "the state of water-in-the-world" as she systematically pours water from a cup into a bowl, onto the floor and then tries to lift the water from the floor back into the cup; or the actions of a child digging in the sand; or helping to sweep the floor; or, when older, taking care of a younger sibling. All these examples are illustrative of work-play at different moments of the child's life, as she engages in social action upon the world that is meaningful and relevant, fulfilling both a personal and social purpose.

The opportunities for meaningful "labor" (so-called) afforded children in socialist societies such as Cuba, Guinea-Bissau, and China, and in Israeli kibbutzim, partially fulfill this work-play dimension in the lives of children; although if this meaningful labor becomes adult-structured, regimented, and coercive, such action loses its expressive character and lapses into the unidimensional definition of "work."

When we critically reflect on the reification of play that has occurred in the early "schooling" of children, we notice not only that natural play has been denied to the child but that play itself has been dichotomized into a structured, cognitive curriculum (which Montessori exponents label "work") and "free play," which is not free but is defined within specific adult-constructed frameworks.

Not only is the child not permitted to experience a fundamental ontological mode, but the very process of play is converted into a false structure of work oriented to the productive functions of the corporate society, where the process of doing is subordinate to the process of producing artifacts. In the first three centers I described (Golda Meir Nursery, Busy Bee Montessori Center, and Lollipop Learning Center, Inc.) children are permitted neither the freedom to play nor the freedom to "work" in a meaningful way; for the work designed by the adult for the child has no relevance beyond its immediate task orientation. The children do not benefit from the fruits of their labor (they do not, for example, eat the vegetables they grow, as a child in an Israeli kibbutz nursery might do), and, most importantly, what they do is not of their own creation. Their work-play actions upon the world are circumscribed by and clash with the demands of the institution which they inhabit.

In our own culture, the Protestant ethic has led us to the peculiar assumption that once elementary schooling begins, schooling must be centered on the world of work, not the world of play. However, prior to this period of schooling, popular notions about the play life of children still do abound, based on the false assumption that children are free of institutional pressures during the early years. Yet the impact of schooling and the Protestant ethic on the very young is a new phenomenon and has not been adequately analyzed by the radical critics and advocates of educational change. The "containment" function of schools that Kozol attacks, the impact of schooling in a corporate society that Carnoy, Gintis, Bowles,[6] and others have documented, the deschooling advocated by Illich,[7] the crisis in the classroom described by Silberman[8]—all refer to a childhood population *beyond* the preschool. What happens when this containment is experienced by two- and three-year-olds? We need to question the impact of the schooling of the "hearts and minds" of several million toddlers and young children in this country and understand the nature of this "ideologization" process.

Space and Time

I did not choose to come into the world, yet once I am born, time flows through me, whatever I do.[9]

Merleau-Ponty describes the experience of time in terms of a field of presence, an abode which we, as body-beings, inhabit. Time is not a progressive seriation of events but arises from our constituted relations with things in the world. Time, as a "network of intentionalities," is integrally linked to our being in the world; the child, as consciousness, constitutes time, and time, in turn, flows through the child.

The primordial experience of this field of presence occurs during infancy, when the child, becoming-in-time, is as yet unaware of the metacategories brought to bear upon lived-time. She does not yet know the exigencies of clock time, and has not yet created the metamodes of objectified, inauthentic time—modes in which we as adults tend to reside, alienated from our temporal beings.

However, the creation of "time-conscious" and, therefore, "time-objectifying" structures which mirror the cultural configurations of alienated time in the macrosocial system erodes the experience of lived-time in young children; for they are socialized into institutional time, where time is no longer a field of presence, an abode, but an austere system of constraints demanding submission. Play is not *part of time*, but *subordinate* to a "planned time" schedule, which determines the spatial and interpersonal modes of existence.

We notice that the temporal mapping of the day that we observed in Golda Meir, Lollipop, and Montessori defined particular spatially selected activities to be performed within certain time "limits" associated with clock time. The function of institutionalized time was evident, for it gave to the staff the powers of prediction and social control which resulted in the refashioning of the child's lived-time world.

In Lollipop Learning Center, with its extreme product orientation, the child's process of doing-in-time was ruthlessly subordinated to the manufacture and production of artifacts. In Busy Bee Montessori, a fetishism of procedure rituals coerced the child to complete one activity in chronological time, prior to engaging in another. The rituals of taking-out work and putting-away work dominated the child's process of doing, which was strictly defined spatially. "Valid" acts only occurred on rugs, designated tables, and in the circle—three spatial extensions within which all movement was contained. In Golda Meir Nursery, the rigid demarcation of the day into temporal slots was internalized by the children, who re-structured their experience to accommodate "free-play time," "hungry time," "singing time," "story time," "going-home time," evincing a fragmented perspective of their daily ex-perience.

The transgression of the temporal and spatial boundaries led, in turn, to the ascription of *deviance*, where the "de-viants" emerged as temporal or spatial norm violators. Only at Martin Luther King Center, where there existed a low bound-ary separation in space and time, were such ascriptions of deviance *not* seen to occur. Thus, to be a "normal" child within the first three centers meant being normal-in-time and normal-in-space according to institutional criteria defined on the basis of the adult "work" world.

The spontaneous, moving, energetic, playing being of the child presented a threat to these organizational structures and hence needed to be contained. The untrained, mischievous toddler constituted a problem because playfulness, physical exploration, and curiosity were anti-norms detrimental to the imposed spatial and temporal structure. Children were not free to create their own landscape; to significantly imprint their mark upon the environment. They were denied their own history-making power, which as *becoming beings* is an existentially vital theme.

In both the Martin Luther King Center and Pine Woods Free School, children *were* permitted to endow their land-scape with significance and, in fact, were actively involved in transforming the nature of their environment. The spatial arrangements at both schools shifted constantly—rooms were rearranged and there was no set position for respective ob-jects. In this way both schools reflected patterns of dis-continuity with the macrosocial system. Martin Luther King, a black low-income school with a distinct set of subcultural characteristics, emerged with a far more integrative, child-oriented landscape than most centers. Pine Woods, ideo-logically committed to the establishment of a countercultural institution, rejected the spatial and temporal organization con-sidered conducive to schooling.

In both these centers, which represented only a small minority of preschools, we see how the play-world of the child emerged against the backdrop of childcare institutions that stood on the margin of society—and, in this sense, were atypical, in both theory and practice, of the dominant ideology of early institutionalization.

Deviance and Authenticity

We have seen that many activities germane to the nature of play are precisely the ones perceived as deviant by childcare staff. Yet if this existential role of play were better appreciated, docile, passive, conforming behavior might be considered "deviant" to the core of childhood.

The child, as a conscious *becoming* being, pursues a "project" of freedom in order to become someone herself and not a being-for-others. This pursuit on the part of the child closely parallels Heidegger's search for "authenticity" and Sartre's *pour-soi/en-soi* modalities. "Neither the wanting-to-be-independently or wanting-to-be-someone himself should be considered as the verbal expression of a value or as an ideal that is consciously held by the child: they are underlying structurations of being-child."[10]

Vandenberg, influenced by Buytendijk,[11] has depicted several phases in the development of experienced freedom in the young child. Of particular significance are the phases of freedom of caprice and initiative. During this period the child explores her world, responding to the provocative qualities that demand something of her. The child's being is projected into the world, while simultaneously adapting to things as experienced. If the child is prohibited from this thrust of freedom, then

> his exercise of freedom of caprice and initiative seems to be the freedom of revolt and refusal. The "negativism" associated with phases of childhood when considered phenomenologically is the irrepressibility of the experience of freedom—of being independently when the child's consciousness has not yet deepened sufficiently to make freedom of conquest or choice possible, he has to be independently anyway. He does this, if necessary, by positing a world of refusal.[12]

In order to discover herself, the child must *rebel.* The popular notion of the "terrible-two tantrums" testifies to a general understanding of this initiation of defiance on the part of the child. The child, in order to discover herself, must experience her world in a dialectical fashion and thereby be permitted the *freedom to disobey;* without that freedom, the child cannot involve herself in ontologically meaningful relations with the world-of-the-other. Her project-for-being must first be experienced prior to appreciating the projects of other beings, and her wanting-to-be-someone herself is the prior condition for subsequent exploration of the world-of-the-other.

Sartre,[13] in his discussion of adult authenticity, depicts the *en-soi/pour-soi* modes of consciousness, housed in a perpetual dialectic. Freedom for Sartre involves transcendence through negation of the inert, passive en-soi mode. "To be truly free then, is to allow the *pour-soi* to cancel the *en-soi* ... to exist beyond and above the past which is the *en-soi.*"[13]

This history-making power of the individual, the transforming nature of one's action upon the social world, arises from the praxis of constituting individuals who are intentionally directed upon the world. To reside in the en-soi mode is thus to live without *directed* intentionality, to constitute without praxis, to have one's being defined by "the other," and to fulfill an inauthentic project for being.

When we consider the lives of children in some of the institutions under study, we are faced with a critical question: Are the staff systematically denying the intentionality of the children? When the intentionality of a child was directed against the structural order, either it was negated or the child was labeled as deviant. Consider Jomo's transgression of sociability and Raina's act of physically overturning the structure in the Montessori center and the labeled children, such as Coleman, Vera, and Shawn in Lollipop Learning Center. In such contexts, we become aware of how *differences are made pathological;* deviance emerges not as a quality intrinsic to an act but as the product of an audience or social definition. Social groups "create deviance by making the rules whose infraction constitutes deviance and by applying those rules to particular people and labeling them as outsiders."[14]

Deviance is therefore seen to represent a social construction of reality imposed by the power elite of the institution, whose goal is structural maintenance, through an effective institutionalization process. The children undergo a "stripping of self" process analogous to that described by Goffman when writing of the inmate world in *Asylums*.[15] This "disculturation" process is a necessary primary adjustment in the closed inmate world. We observed a similar process taking place in the Montessori training period and in the punitive environment of the profit daycare. The child that breaks the residual rules, that emerges as incompletely socialized, is ascribed labels of "troublemaker," "nonworker," "problematical," "learning-disabled," and "hyperactive"; her failure to conform to object, spatial, and temporal norms is translated into a disease paradigm of mental pathology and deviance.

At this point, we note how the pathology of the social institution in question is neatly reversed to encapsulate an intrapsychic diagnosis, and we witness a blaming-of-the-victim syndrome.[16] No longer need one question the existential landscape, the social milieu into which the child is inserted. Instead, a reductionistic set of categories are imposed, which locate the problem within the being of the child, not within the forms of the institutionalization process. The child is caught in a severe double bind: to be herself authentically as part of her "structurated" child-being is to be at once deviant; to be for the institution is not to be. *The being of childhood is thus seen to be antithetical to the life of the institution.*

The "Ideologization" of Childhood: Education as Domestication

It follows logically from the banking notion of consciousness that the educator's role is to regulate the way the world "enters into" the students. His task is to organize a process which already occurs spontaneously, to "fill" the students by making deposits

of information which he considers to constitute
true knowledge . . . The educated man is the adapted
man because he is better "fit" for the world. Translated into practice, this concept is well suited to the
purposes of the oppressors, whose tranquility rests
on how well men fit the world the oppressors have
created, and how little they question it.[17]

Freire contrasts the banking concept of education with that of
the "problematizing," dialogical encounter. In the former
process the teacher performs a narrative role, depositing information in the assumed tabula rasa mind of the student. The
content of this narration is not germane to the student but detached from the reality of the existential landscape. The more
completely students accept the passive role imposed upon
them, the more they tend to adapt to the world *as is* and to the
reductionistic view of reality deposited in them. Authentic
pedagogy, claims Freire, does not lie in modes of domestication which involve accommodation to the structures of oppression. A liberating pedagogy transforms the structures of oppression by awakening critical consciousness in students.

The difference between the banking concept of education
and the dialogical encounter is that the former anesthetizes
creativity and critical thought, while the latter relies on
problematizing, on a continual confrontation between the individual and the sociopolitical cultural reality.

In the childhood analogue to Freire's adult pedagogy, the
child that does not "fit" the preschool structure becomes a
deviant; the child who moves beyond the planned deposits of
the "narrating teacher" and restructures an activity frequently
encounters reprimand and retraining. The curious, inventive
mind of the child is actively socialized into docility and
passivity by the schooling staff, who thus emerge as oppressors of the child's freedom to develop her being.

During the preschool years, which roughly correspond to
the late sensorimotor and preoperational stages of development, the child is involved in the active exploration of her
world which Piaget claims is fundamental to the development
of thought. It is through the child's process of self-discovery
that mature conceptual operations arise. It is action that forms

the basis for thought. By depriving the child of her spontaneous, inherent curiosity, we deprive the child of her right to invent. We can train the child to "learn" particular isolated facts through repeated deposits of information, but that fact will always remain an isolated fact closed in, and of itself, closed to integration and understanding, for, as Piaget points out, "Programmed instruction is indeed conducive to learning, but by no means to inventing."[18]

In many preschools I observed, children were expected to "learn" content unrelated to their developmental and interest levels; freedom of exploration was systematically negated, and invention in the artifactual world was prevented by the ascribed unidimensionality of objects. There was little encouragement for the child to integrate her understanding into the structures of the becoming self. We witness, instead, the bureaucratization of knowledge. "Given the functions of preventing internal change and struggling to survive, bureaucracies tend to devote much of their time to activities that will prevent change."[19]

The child who is in active pursuit of understanding her world, the child who is creative and inventive, who sees the multifaceted possibilities inherent in a blackboard eraser (cf. Molly's deviance in Busy Bee Montessori), the child whose energy will not be contained, the child who plays—a child such as this constitutes a threat to the knowledge bureaucracy which has been transposed upon the child's landscape. The planned curriculum must be maintained; the schedule must be strictly adhered to; the cognitive learning environment must be kept constant. Within this order paradigm the child who is docile and obedient depicts functional adaptation; the child who is playful becomes maladaptive, a threat, and an interloper to the carefully contoured experiences of her agemates. Conflict is thus seen as dysfunctional, as detrimental to the order and stability of the environment. Children need to be socialized "to follow directions," and the structure of the landscape is geared to the minimization of interpersonal conflict and the avoidance of spatial and temporal dislocation. This is mediated by a powerful system of controls whereby the school's state of health is seen to rest upon an outer structure of calm, harmony, and adjustment. One of the characteristics of an equilibrium institution such as the school is an inherent rigidity, an inability to accommodate change, which results in spatial, temporal, or interpersonal dislocation.

We saw this structural rigidity in Golda Meir Nursery, Busy Bee Montessori, and Lollipop Learning Center, along with the corresponding patterns of staff interaction which denied the intentionality of the child and prevented the expression of anger or the experience of conflict. At Martin Luther King, by contrast, there was an easy toleration of conflict as "natural for kids that age." Conflict was not separated out from the lived experience, but was considered inherent in the daily fabric of existence. The ease with which conflict was tolerated was inextricably tied to the subcultural tradition to which these children and staff were linked, whose own history bore witness to conflict and struggle and not to order and social equilibrium.

What relevance do these sociological models hold for understanding the context of life in a preschool? They are, after all, merely metaconstructions, once removed from the life-world; yet I believe that the choice, conscious or unconscious, of paradigms for viewing the features of a schooling experience directs our attention in such a way that we look at the same presenting features through a different lens.

> The conflict and order models understand the same phenomena differently, stress different system dynamics, and would even have us attend to different issues and gather different data. One poignant example is the differing understandings of conflict provided by the two models. The order model sees conflict as a dysfunction which threatens systemic integration necessary for the system to provide for the "well-being of all" its members. In contrast, the conflict model sees "well-being of all" as a euphemism for control and elite privilege. It views conflict as a healthy manifestation of the system's difficulty in meeting individual and group needs, and as a vital source of energy, ideas and constituency to achieve change.[20]

Very rarely, in my observations, was the child who behaved aggressively understood in relation to the school structure (or lack thereof). In all the centers described in the preceding chapters, the staff saw aggression as part of the children's development. Dependent on the respective schooling ideology, aggression was viewed as something to be controlled or expressed, eradicated or tolerated. The child's actions were rarely understood, however, as a call to the teachers to reexamine their own inadequate response to the children's needs or to change the learning environment or classroom structure in order to challenge the children in more constructive ways.[21]

Psychology, too, couched within a sociological model of equilibrium, has developed theories pertaining to the expression of rebellion and aggression. While Freud claimed that psychoanalysis was devoid of any Weltanschauung, it does embrace a view of social reality oriented to an equilibrium perspective. The principal of homeostasis has emerged as an integral part of psychodynamics. Socialization theory has espoused the training of disruptive impulses, with disruption viewed from the perspective of the smooth-functioning social structure. An adjustment norm in therapy has oriented the individual to change in order to accommodate to the status quo of the structure.

This unidimensional view of the young child points to the need for a dialectical psychology which, claims Klaus Riegel, would shift the emphasis from studies that focus on the tranquillity of the mind and the social order, on individual adjustment and system maintenance, to the far more complex analysis of how problems are created, order disturbed, and contradictions posed.[22]

My intent is not to advance the belief that the young child's expression of aggression is necessarily positive, nor that aggression should freely be expressed in an unbounded environment; rather, I have attempted to elucidate the dominant equilibrium Weltanschauung within which the order ideology of "schooling" is located. By understanding the social context of such a paradigm, it is hoped that the current perception of aggression and conflict within the preschool will be recognized and critically examined; for this perception of social conflict is geared toward a nondialectical view of human experience. Both poles of the dialectic need to be acknowledged: freedom to love and to hate, to obey and to disobey. "The paradoxical element in the grounding of educating is that the child has to be free to disobey in order to genuinely obey . . . To suggest that there has to be room for disobedience, then, places freedom in dialectical relation rather than in opposition to pedagogic authority."[23]

Freedom to disobey, freedom to conflict, does not suggest the creation of a limitless laissez-faire environment, as was often observed in Pine Woods Free School. The dialectical antithesis to child oppression is another form of oppression; for then the child has no structure of authority against which to rebel, no means of asserting her pour-soi. A limitless situation throws the child into nothingness and does not aid in the humanization of the life-world of the child, for she then lacks the solidity of being. What *is* needed, however, is a flexible understanding of this dialectical experience in child-life.

An authentic existential landscape permits the child to experience the dialectic of life—the dialectic of structure and freedom. In this, the child may be allowed to experience conflict, to express aggression, to experience the freedom to disobey, but be bounded by the awareness-of-the-other, awake to the possibility of disapproval and reprimand. The dialectic of conflict is such that it can be a positive bonding experience from which much learning and empathy-for-the-other may emerge. In addition, to be in conflict means that one must invent new modes. To be in harmony means that one can exist without awareness. One needs to stand on the edge of the dialectic to profit from its power.[24]

The Childcare Industry

The only type of personality the school can support
and approve is one that fits smoothly into the institutional organization . . . The type of personality
needed in the school is the same as that needed in
the corporation.[25]

In addressing the political economy of schooling, a critical examination of the link between corporate capitalism and the social context of schooling becomes necessary.

Spring, Gintis and Bowles have incisively demonstrated, through their historical and political analyses, how the evolution of the school in the United States had little to do with equality and much to do with meeting the needs of capitalist employers for a disciplined and skilled labor force.[26] The school, claimed Bowles, provided a mechanism for social and political control; for the inequalities in the school system have served increasingly to reproduce the class structure from one generation to another. The social relations of work have replicated the social relations of the school, specifically in the areas of discipline, punctuality, acceptance of authority outside the family, and conformity.

In the capitalist economy, one's status, income, and personal autonomy depend increasingly upon one's status in the hierarchy of work relations. We see the very same trend mirrored in the school tracking system where the so-called "unbiased," "objective" test instruments divide those that have internalized the corporate value system and efficiency concepts from those that have not—where the true function of the IQ becomes one that legitimates the social institutions, which underpin the stratification system.[27]

While these theorists argue that a critical analysis should be applied to the political organization of the school, the school as such is still viewed as a formal institution. Since schooling no longer begins at six years, however, but in late infancy, we now witness the transposition of a corporate model from the formal maintenance institution—the. school—to the informal maintenance institution—the preschool.

With the rapid rise of the daycare movement over the past decade and the inevitable absorption of women into a corporate economy, attendant modes of alienation have been produced by a bureaucratically-organized hierarchical division of labor, where the female "worker" now occupies the lowest echelon of power and status. The current call for free and universal daycare should not be viewed as a progressive or radical answer to the social needs of women in a society entering the work force seeking the equalization of opportunity; rather, the daycare phenomenon merely extends and exascerbates the corporate paradigm, thereby contributing to the *maintenance,* not the *transformation* of the social order. The most telling example of this phenomenon is the translation of daycare into a profitable industry, exemplified by the burgeoning number of profit and franchise daycare centers

that have sprung up across the country. Mary Moppets
(Southwest), American Child Centers (Kentucky), Kay's Kid-
die Kollege (Florida), and Universal Education Corporation
(East Coast) represent some of the largest corporations. Yet the
"business of young children is growth and development and
the business of corporations is making money. If you mix the
two, can the needs of both be satisfied? Will look-alike child
centers inevitably turn out look-alike children?"[28] Consider
the following description extracted from the reports of a visitor
to Mary Moppets' Daycare Center in Arizona.

> The Moppets Center I visited remains open from 6:30 A.M.
> until 1:30 A.M. six days a week. It is licensed for fifty chil-
> dren and they come and go constantly. The children don't
> know one another and the teachers don't know them.
>   When I arrived at 9:00 A.M., the two teachers caring for
> thirty children appeared frenzied. They swept the floor,
> picked up broken crayons, lugged around a wailing child,
> rushed a toddler to the toilet. A few youngsters, thumbs in
> mouth, watched television. Others played desultorily with
> toys stocked in half-empty cupboards. A few toyed with the
> buckle on my shoe. One two-year-old just whimpered.[29]

While Mary Moppets is a twelve-franchise corporation
situated in the Southwest, staffed by middle management and
directed by a corporate executive, the core quality experience
shadows many of the themes that emerged from my observations at Lollipop Learning Center, Inc.

Consider yet another series of observations on profit-run
centers cited in Mary Keyserling's *Windows on Daycare.*

> If ever there was a way to close a day care center, this one
> should be the first to go. The proprietor is not interested in
> child care, but only in making a profit. She wants to get out
> of the business and will sell to anyone who will buy it. Back
> in a dark room, a baby was strapped in an infant's seat in-
> side a crib and was crying pitifully.[30]

Or yet another snapshot:

> Very poor basement dark room. All ages together. Rigid
> control and discipline. Run-down equipment. This is a sad
> case of inhumane dehumanizing of kids by an owner who
> makes plenty of money.[31]

The insignificance of the child in these "childcare" institutions is alarming. It is clear that the business of childcare negates the being of the child, who emerges as the voiceless and helpless victim of a growing industry which is manipulating the child as a profit integer in the services of the corporate enterprise. The child becomes objectified because it is not the human development of the child that is fostered, but rather, how many children can be contained within the structure for the greatest amount of money and smallest number of staff. It is under those conditions that a profit turnover can be increased and it is these very conditions which produce fragmentation, hostility, violence and severe forms of alienation, contributing to the overwhelming experience of anomie within the life-world of the child, such as we have seen at Lollipop Learning Center, Inc., and its many counterparts across the country.

If childhood, as a life phase, is a "becoming at home in the world," the *homelessness* of the children in these hostile and unfriendly institutions is sad testimony to the erosion of childhood.

10
Toward the Deinstitutionalization of Childhood

This is the place to start, for that is where the children are. For only a hard look at the world in which they live—a world we adults have created for them in large part by default—can convince us of the urgency of their plight and the consequences of our inaction. Then perhaps it will come to pass that, in the words of Isaiah, "A little child shall lead them."
Urie Bronfenbrenner
TWO WORLDS OF CHILDHOOD[1]

The world in which children live—the institutional world that babies, toddlers, and the very young have increasingly come to inhabit and confront—is a world in which they have become the objects, not the subjects of history, a world in which *history is being made of them.* "One of the most striking characteristics of our time is the fact that history is made without self-awareness."[2] This deficient awareness, this forgetfulness of the *being* of childhood is indicative of a far-reaching "social amnesia"[3] that permeates our narcissistic culture today.

It would be easy to lay the blame for the erosion of childhood squarely at the feet of the daycare movement; but that is too simplistic a solution for a much more complex set of issues for which the crisis in daycare has become both symptom and scapegoat.

The way in which a society cares, or does not care, for its young is indicative of its own vitality and social fabric; and when both the young and the old are relegated to age-segregated institutions so as to focus exclusively on the "productive prime" of adulthood, the sanity and wisdom of such actions bear scrutiny. "If the current trend persists, if the institutions of our society continue to remove parents, other adults and older youth from active participation in the lives of children, and if the resulting vacuum is filled by the age-segregated peer group, *we can anticipate increased alienation, indifference, antagonism, and violence on the part of the younger generation in all segments of our society.*"[4] Why do we continue to remove children from the center of our lives and relegate them to the confines of the age-segregated institution? The answers may lie beyond the scope of this book in a penetrating analysis of the effects of modernity and the social alienation that results from the technologization of the human consciousness, for the ideas, judgments, beliefs, and myths of our modern milieu[5] have been uprooted and modified in the shadow of the technological image. It is easy, with this "focalistic vision," to fragment our lived experience, to atomize our perceptions of reality, to compartmentalize generations of children and adults from each other, and ultimately to create ahistorical individuals, disconnected from the history of their own childhood and the future of their own children.

It is into this shadow of social amnesia that the experts on childraising, early childhood education, child development, and child morality step, swiftly and impersonally with brisk precision, diagnosing, and thereby cementing, the cracks in the edifice of anomie, never pausing to question the structures of separateness engendered by the deficient technical consciousness of our current milieu.

The bitter experience of oppression that women have endured and the social dislocation resulting from the struggle for liberation, have called forth an even more separatist era—an era dominated in toto by adulthood. At the extreme side of this separatist era we have Shulamit Firestone espousing her "radical" technological vision of "cybernetic socialism," which, she claims, must of necessity lead to the demise of childhood.[6] While Firestone's radical "adultist" vision is not shared by many of the participants in the women's movement, the expedient notion of the child as a commodity to be dispensed with and deposited in impersonal or inadequate childcare institutions shows how this "commoditization" of

childhood has taken us further along the path of social alienation.

As we have seen in many early childhood institutions, the
lives of children do not really matter. But we should consider
what happens to those lives when, from babyhood, the institution replaces the parents and family as the primary
socializer. Berger and Luckmann discuss the formation of a
"reflected self" (à la Mead and Cooley) and the importance of
emotional attachment, as the child, through identification with
intimate significant others and the internalization of roles and
attitudes, develops an identity: "The child does not internalize the world of his significant others as one of many possible worlds. He internalizes it as *the* world, the only existent
and only conceivable world, the world *tout court*."[7] But what
if the primary socialization experience occurs in a world
where the child is insignificant, has no consistent significant
others, and where a changing turnover of caregivers, a series
of transitory faces, come and go? What is entrenched in consciousness when the internalization of institutional "sub-
worlds"[8] becomes a primary as opposed to a secondary
socialization process? For if the individual's first world, during this early period of primary identity formation, is constructed within an alien set of interpersonal encounters in
which neither the child nor the adult become the reciprocal
significant other, we realize that to be given an identity in
such a context does not involve "being assigned a specific
place in the world"[9] at all. Rather, the children are disconnected from the alien institutional universe to which they
do not belong and become the actors upon a "home-less" and
barren stage; for they are deprived of their human vocation as
meaning-makers. If my interpretation of the experiences of
children in the institutions described in part 2 of this book is
accurate, we need to ask whether the children and child institutions are not, at present, dialectically juxtaposed in a
series of unremitting contradictions. If so, what critical issues,
what alternative paths and possibilities for the deinstitutionalization of the very young should be considered?

Women and Children

One of the painful paradoxes of the women's liberation movement is that the quest for human rights has resulted in the oppression of children; for the pursuit for liberation has often been waged at the cost of the early "containment" of children.

Yet the demand of the movement for free and universal day-care for poor and middle-class women alike does not necessarily represent all women's aspirations. In this country, "women's lib" has been a largely middle-class movement, controlled and supported in the main by women who choose to work, to follow career goals, and to pursue higher education, as opposed to the historical necessity of women who *had* to work out of sheer economic privation but who would not necessarily *choose* to work. Free and universal daycare may meet the childcare needs of both classes of women, but the assumption that all women want to work in a productive function outside the home is clearly not shared by many working-class women; for their very work only serves to further perpetuate their economic and social oppression. This class dilemma is effectively captured by the "maid-missus" dialogue in Robert and Jane Coles's *Women of Crisis*, as we listen to the maid talking.

> Women like me go to work because we "have" to; there's no alternative but living poorer lives. None of my friends want to go to that factory . . . I worry about my own children while I take care of other people's children. That's the way it has to be, I know. I need the money. They have the money . . . ! If I had money, I'd quit this job, and go home and stay home for a thousand years. I'd be with my own kids and not someone else's. Does it make sense? The missus says that she has to get out and work, or else she'll "stagnate"—her favorite word. She's always worrying about stagnating. She says women are in danger of "stagnating." Maybe in her dictionary I'm not a woman![10]

These comments, by the maid of an upper-class woman in Cambridge, Massachusetts, mirror the paradoxes and double oppression that is perpetuated by a women's liberation movement in a class-stratified society. The pursuit of libera-

tion by the "missus," in this case, is dependent upon the oppression of another woman who becomes the traditional
domestic figure of the household, in which female oppression
is still perpetuated by one class of women upon another. The
"second" woman experiences this double oppression both at
the hands of her female employer and of her husband at home
(although she may not perceive the latter role as oppressive).
Her children are also oppressed in this cycle of hierarchical
domestication; for they must either be cared for by *another*
woman or be shunted off to a childcare institution; and, as the
field of possibilities is often closed or, at best, limited, the
chances of finding a center *unlike* Lollipop Learning Center,
Inc., are not very great when one is poor and desperate for
childcare.

Such women are caught in a double bind, and their plight is
widespread among both poor working women and women on
welfare. Selma Fraiberg depicts the situation as "the Looking
Glass World of Day Care in which hundreds of thousands of
mothers on welfare take care of the children of hundreds of
thousands of working mothers and other mothers on welfare,
while hundreds of thousands of women take care of the children of the mothers who are taking care of the children of
mothers on welfare and other mothers!"[11] It is patently clear
that the absurdity of the situation described above is not a
metaphor for liberation. The condition of poor women is very
different from that of middle-class women; the divisions are
great, the aspirations are often diametrically opposed. Yet in
both cases the children suffer because there is no adequate
and articulated philosophy and practice of childcare in this
country; and, as is customary in a class-based society, it is the
poor who suffer most from the consequences. While the
middle-class woman follows her career aspirations, demanding a system of universally available childcare, the economic
and social stratification system that exists will continue to ensure differential freedoms based on class and sex privilege.
Confronted by this universe of themes, which are in dialectical contradiction, women "take equally contradictory po-
sitions, some work to maintain the structures, others to change
them. As antagonism deepens between the themes which are

the expression of reality, there is a tendency for the themes and for reality itself to be mythicized."[12]

The themes in need of demystification that Freire speaks of, are those that attempt to maintain the current structures of domination, where the palliative solutions of the middle class and well-off are not necessarily those of the poor; for it is only in a socio-political transformation that the seeds of liberation for both women and children can take place.

> I consider the fundamental theme of our epoch to be that of domination—which implies its opposite, the theme of liberation, as the objective to be achieved. It is this tormenting theme which gives our epoch the anthropological character mentioned earlier. In order to achieve humanization, which presupposes the elimination of dehumanizing oppression, it is absolutely necessary to surmount the limit-situations.[13]

In order to transcend the "limit-situations" that are integral to our corporate technological era, seeds of resistance to the current massification of children must be sown by broadening our consciousness about other forms of life for children and taking action in such directions.

Some Cross-Cultural Snapshots

In looking at how other countries outside of the United States have taken care of their young, there is much to learn and much to criticize.

Unlike this country, socialist societies have invested an enormous amount of commitment and energy in the task of caring for and educating their young. While early institutionalization still presents problems, some of the most negative and debilitating aspects of that process are countervailed by the attempt to create a positive collective institutional experience for the child who will become the "new man" or the "new woman."

In Cuba, for example, the children are seen as the prime movers of the future society—and early childhood education is viewed as an integral component of the process of social transformation, which is designed to liberate the Cuban woman from the exploitation and chauvinism of the past.[14] Women in the new society are viewed as indispensable to social and economic development, and their necessary inclusion in the labor force has required a comprehensive childcare system freely available to the children of working mothers. As a result, the Federation of Cuban Women administers an impressive array of preschool programs, which provide health services, nutrition, and daily care for infants from forty-five days to five years, allowing mothers to leave home and work in the factories, in the fields, and in the various professions. Most centers remain open from 6 A.M. to 6 P.M., six days a week. A few operate as residential nurseries where infants board during the week, only returning home on weekends. It appears that, despite the social transformation that has taken place, prevailing stereotypes of women still exist, for it is women who exclusively staff the centers, and very few role/occupational changes are evident in the society. Neither does there appear to be sufficient critical examination of the early separation of the infant from the family, and the potentially harmful effects of a sixty-to-seventy-hour-a-week institutional experience.

The task of the schools, including the early childhood centers, is that of "painting appropriate images of the new society in the child's mind"[15] and making that environment instrumental in developing new perspectives. "Cuban educators believe they can develop a new consciousness among nursery school children. By weaving into the curriculum and the everyday classroom life such concepts and behavioral patterns as sharing, respect for work, responsibility, modesty, and self-discipline, Cuban educators feel they can assist in the creation of the new Cuban man."[16]

There is a strong emphasis on the development of an antiegoist psychology, and most activities are designed to stimulate group play, in which the *asistentes* lead children to social and play patterns that develop collective attitudes. Babies are placed in collective playpens or corrals where, for example, six infants will be encouraged to experience face-to-face interaction in a shared social space.

In Leiner's detailed account of the *circulos*,[17] as well as the philosophically more permissive *jardines*, we view the negative problems associated with the early institutionalization of the young. Yet we realize that there *does* exist, through the emphasis on collective attitudes and social cooperation, a more child-sensitive environment. Cuban childcare centers encourage families to participate in school affairs and offer intensive courses on childraising. Outside organizations (farms, factories, offices) adopt the circulos and provide supportive services—all of which help to educate the family and community on the importance of the child to Cuban society.

Similarly, in China during the Mao Tse-tung period, the early education of children was viewed as a means for instilling the correct *moral*, *physical*, and *intellectual* development in order to carry the revolution forward into the future. For genuine equality between the sexes to occur, women needed to be free to join in productive activity; so babies were accepted from fifty-six days into the feeding stations, attached to the mother's workplace. As most infants were nursed until their first birthday, mothers were permitted to feed their babies twice during their work shift.

Ruth Sidel, in a generally favorable account of the Chinese childcare system, reports that multiple rather than serial mothering was the norm, whereby infants were able to form stable relationships with their caregiver "aunties." "We were repeatedly told that 'aunties' and teachers rarely leave their jobs. And they are warm and loving with the children. The children show none of the lethargy or other intellectual, emotional, or physical problems of institutionalized children. Quite the opposite."[18]

However, an American team of child researchers who visited China in 1973 reported some disturbing observations. Caregivers, while described as warm and gentle, rarely held or touched the infants and discouraged free mobility. Since floors were cold and rooms small, neither crawling nor walking was freely permitted. The research team found that "children under three years of age, at least in the presence of strange visitors, were quiet and affectively subdued."[19] Little playful interaction between adults and children or between children was reported. Because toys were considered unimportant in the developmental process, few were available. Caregivers described infants as dependent, helpless, and relatively inactive—and the institutional stress on hygiene and careful feeding resulted in scant attention to sensory or intellectual stimulation. This contrasted with the picture of the kindergarten children (three to seven years) where "the difference between the expressive, well organized, socially adept four year olds, and the immobile, shy and almost expressionless toddlers just thirty feet down the hall was dramatic."[20] The kindergarten children were strikingly competent in art and in musical dance routines, and their self-control, discipline, and concentration differed markedly from their American counterparts. They also engaged in productive labor; each kindergarten organized its own factory, and age-appropriate tasks were given to the children (such as fitting light bulbs into cartons). Many other centers cultivated vegetable gardens. All these activities took place in a tightly organized structure with no element of choice and few free-play opportunities. All activities appeared to be teacher-initiated—designed to promote *moral, physical,* and *intellectual* development—the three central principles of the educational process. The concept of the child as initiator and actor was absent.

An even more rigid institutional experience is found in the "Sovietization of childhood." Bronfenbrenner reports on the "scientific" attitude to the collectivization of Soviet children and the docile conforming behavior produced.[21] In some ways, this presents an extreme version of the bureaucratization of experience observed in a Montessori education, but in making such cross-cultural comparisons we realize the bewildering complexity of nuances and cultural epistemologies that cannot easily be comprehended by an outsider. As Bronfenbrenner rightly points out, there are "two worlds of childhood." These two worlds carry correspondingly different ideas about the nature and forms of childhood. Furthermore, when images of children are tied to the expedient necessities of states undergoing a social and political transformation, we are confronted by a dual problem of interpretation—the adult as well as the Western lens.

In two postrevolutionary societies in Africa, Guinea-Bissau and Mozambique, the protracted liberation struggles led to a radical examination of the traditional African woman's position of servitude in a colonial society.[22] If the traditional patriarchal African family structure was to be superseded by a more egalitarian one, both adult women and their older daughters (who had previously served as infant caregivers) would have access to training and a life outside the home. In both these societies, plans are underway to set up work centers for women (in rural communal villages) with childcare centers attached. However, despite the attempts to end discrimination against women, advocated by Samora Machel and the late Amilcar Cabral,[23] the sexual division of labor still continues in the home with women assuming major responsibility for childcare and the household, in addition to their work outside the home.

How the young will fare in all these societies is an open question, and whether the commitment to the formation of the new man and the new woman will also result in the formation of the new child under socialism is open to speculation and ongoing review until further in-depth investigations are available. On the one hand, children do become history-makers; they do engage in meaningful play-work (in the form of productive labor); they are viewed as the treasures, the flowers of the new society, to be carefully cultivated and tended. Much of the social planning is oriented to the welfare and needs of *all* the children, particularly the poor who suffered the most under the old regimes. On the other hand, children in such societies, like many in the United States, often undergo intense institutional lives; they are subject to tight discipline, varying degrees of rigidly structured programs, and little social space to freely play and experiment with their world.

It is interesting, in the context of this discussion, that the early institutionalization of children has been a controversial issue in Czechoslovakia[24] in recent years. A leading Czech pediatrician, Maria Damborská, has questioned the wisdom of institutional experiences for the under-threes. She claims that the noise, the constant crying, and the long hours spent in a group affects the child's nervous system. The problems posed by forcing young children to wake early, their experiences of frequent stranger anxiety, their lack of consistent interplay with an adult while learning to speak, the divided authority between the home and the center, all lead Dr. Damborská and other influential Czech experts to advocate more time spent at home or in a family setting, fewer hours at the center, and a more gradual transition from home to the institution in the early years.

The Israeli kibbutz nursery, in existence for over four decades, stands somewhere between the rigid Russian institution and the less formal Cuban centers. These group-reared children are not subjected to serial mothering but are nurtured and mothered by a familiar *metapelet* who encourages peer rather than adult dependency and a collective upbringing. As work on the kibbutz stops at 3:00 P.M., parents are free to be with their children from 3:00 to 7:00 each day. Bettelheim's 1969 study of a kibbutz indicates that the early years of the children were difficult, but by age six they seemed to have adjusted, and he concludes that the kibbutz did produce a healthy personality, with less emphasis on personal identity, emotional intimacy, and individual achievement—all adaptive to kibbutz life. The key to this social development, Bettelheim surmises, lay in the replacement of the parents by the peer group as the object of deep early attachment bonds. However, he does claim that from the period of adolescence and beyond they encountered difficulty in forming intimate relationships.[25]

The kibbutz is notably different from previous examples, in that historically the nursery has been a part of the kibbutz, not apart from it; most parents work on the kibbutz—a closed agricultural community which is cohesive and stable, and the nursery becomes part of the familiar horizons of the child's world. In this sense, while still a preschool institution, it is less alienating than the centers of the other countries previously described. It is the "children's place," and that may lessen the institutional impact on its young charges. In recent years, however, more parents have been employed outside the kibbutz, and childrearing practices are in flux, allowing children in many communities to sleep at home with their families. These changes are bound to affect the life-world experiences of the children.

Sweden may offer the best model of an innovative childcare system that bridges the ideological gulf and the different images of childhood that separate the United States from both

Eastern European countries and the Third World. In Sweden, both mothers and fathers are entitled to take maternity or paternity leave, which for the first nine months can be split between the two parents. If the leave-taking parent worked prior to the birth of the child, a guaranteed income (90 percent of one's salary) and a job to return to are ensured. In addition, if a parent wishes to remain home for an additional three months (until the child is a year old), he or she may do so without pay, but with a daily subsidy for the child (the equivalent of about nine dollars a day).

While it is still predominantly women who take paid maternity leave after childbirth, over the last three years the number of fathers taking such leave has risen from 5 to 9 percent. Childcare is accessible and available in neighborhood-based centers which serve specified geographical areas, where every family that uses the center, according to income, pays a proportion of the cost from a bare minimum to half the cost of the care. There has also been an attempt, since 1973, to increase the number of men working in childcare settings, unlike the socialist societies described earlier, where childcare is still "women's work." Several other innovative features of the Swedish system include cross-age mixing of children and the use of the daycare center for instruction in the primary immigrant language—for Sweden has a steady stream of immigrants arriving from Finland, Eastern Europe, and Southern Europe. Here, considerable sensitivity is shown to the developmental needs of the child, who is allowed to live and play in his own language within the childcare center.[26]

In countries we have been discussing, the education and social life of very young children are placed at the center, rather than the periphery, of national priorities. Daycare serves as a means toward the development of the society. In the United States, daycare serves as a means of placing children "in storage," and little attention has been devoted to the results of either mass daycare or profit daycare. We do see, however, that the negative consequences of early institutionalization have not often been critically addressed by socialist states. While the national childcare services are crucial to adult equality in these societies, they are not always in the best interests of the children. How, then, can we achieve

deinstitutionalization in the United States without compromis-
ing either the woman or her child?

Toward the Deinstitutionalization of Early Childhood

I believe that the issue of deinstitutionalization must take account of what Urie Bronfenbrenner has called "encounters of
the fourth kind."[27] Two propositions are central: First, in
order to develop normally, the child needs the *irrational*
involvement of one or more adults—"Someone needs to be
crazy about the child." Second, public and social policy must
provide support time for parenting, for if everyone works full
time, asks Bronfenbrenner, how do you keep a society going?
The critical features of a human ecology must be taken into
account if the social fabric of the society is not to be further
unraveled. At present the process of making children human is
disintegrating, claims Bronfenbrenner, as the rise of maternal
employment is *not* counterbalanced by fathers taking greater
household or parenting responsibilities. In addition, children's lives, particularly poor children's lives, under the
Reagan administration stand in jeopardy, as the existing social
welfare system is dismantled in favor of what is euphemisti-
cally termed "putting the country back to work again."

The possibilities for change, however, do take root, first and
foremost in the family structure, where a democratization of
labor and childcare needs to occur, where the sex-role hier-
archies and domestic division of labor must be equalized and
sanctioned financially by the workplace, the state, and the
federal government. The Swedish model, here, is exemplary:
a guaranteed income and job remove the pressures of institutionalization from a very young infant and his parents.

In this country, the possibility of a guaranteed income or
radical income redistribution plan which favors the poor and
does away with the debilitating welfare rolls would do much
to alleviate the desperate situation of many working mothers
who work because *they have to* in order to survive materially,
and put their children "in storage" not because *they want to*
but because they have no alternative.

Moreover, in the area of childcare it is the task of those who *do* care about the early lives of young children to set up informal, "child-friendly,"[28] cooperative childcare centers that belong to the parents and the children of a given community. These would incorporate elements of the workplace, of the home, of the old and the young, so as to become something of another home—an extended family where grandparents (such as at the Martin Luther King Center) are also part of the childcare landscape, and where a support system can be provided for parents with infants too young to attend. These small, parent-controlled cooperatives are in existence now,[29] but unfortunately are too few and far between. In such centers the institution itself has been deinstitutionalized; it is both *of* the people and fashioned *by* the people, and incorporates teachers as well as parents, children, and older citizens, molding their community to meet their changing needs in a grassroots, nonhierarchical, consensual manner. In such environments, parents as well as "significant others" take part in their young children's early lives. Frequently, both mothers and fathers are required to participate. They function as assistant teachers and surrogate parents. These centers often become the kernel of a community and address other social/political needs that extend beyond childcare—nutrition, ecology, cooperative sharing of resources, etc.

Ideally, such cooperatives should be small—fifteen to twenty families—situated in neighborhood communities, and should receive state and federal subsidies. Teachers in these settings, in the spirit of egalitarianism, should receive appropriate salaries that give full recognition to their significant pedagogic task. At present, early childhood education is one of the lowest-paid professions, and low rather than high status is accorded to this vital work. Parents of children of preschool age should receive mandatory pay and relief from their work responsibilities, for four to five hours "commitment time" at the center per week. Such an environment would not set the child in dialectical contradiction to the institution; for it would be child-centered and embedded in the everyday life of the community.

In this way, that which is often an alien universe to the child becomes a *friendly landscape, grounded in the familiar geog-*

raphy of his lived-world. It is then that childhood becomes a life phase in which everyone, young and old, participates; where children, together with their parents, participate not in an age-segregated institution but in a family community. With the aging Marx we may realize that "this microscopic world is often much more interesting than the macroscopic,"[30] and that in this very microscopic world lies our human life project. It is the children, not alien institutional structures of the corporate or bureaucratic world, who can best teach us how to design intimate childcare landscapes that do not erode their life-world.

Childhood and adulthood constitute the primordial dialectic of our human experience. It is in this generational interplay that our future praxis will be forged as we struggle to recreate a vision of childcare for our time.

Notes

Chapter 1

1. Philippe Ariès, *Centuries of Childhood—A Social History of Family Life* (New York: Knopf, 1962), p. 33. I have borrowed the title "The Idea of Childhood" from part one of *Centuries of Childhood*.

2. Ibid., p. 32.

3. Robert Coles began his address, "Children as Moral Observers," for the Annual Tanner Lecture Series at the University of Michigan, Ann Arbor, 9 April 1980, with these words.

4. Lloyd DeMause, "The Evolution of Childhood," in *The History of Childhood*, ed. Lloyd DeMause (New York: The Psychohistory Press, 1974), p. 1.

5. Ibid., p. 5.

6. Peter Laslett, *The World We Have Lost* (New York: Scribner, 1965), pp. 104–5.

7. Mary Martin McLaughlin, "Survivors and Surrogates," in DeMause, *History of Childhood*, p. 102.

8. DeMause explains these terms in the following way: The *projective reaction:* the adult uses the child as a vehicle for projection of the contents of his unconscious. The *reversal reaction:* the adult uses the child as a substitute for an important adult figure in his own childhood. The *empathic reaction:* the adult empathizes with the child's needs and acts to satisfy them—this last reaction is discussed as a modern-day phenomenon. See "Evolution of Childhood," p. 6.

9. Swaddling appears to have been a near universal practice; where infants were encased so tightly in bandages that their limbs were totally deprived of movement. The flesh was very tightly compressed and gangrene sometimes resulted. Frequently, after being tied up in this way so as to be unable to crawl like an animal on all fours, the child would be hung like a parcel on a peg on the wall, placed in a

tub, or left in a convenient corner. Throwing the swaddled child was also practiced. Indeed, a brother to King Henry IV, being tossed from one window to another in sport, was dropped and killed. See DeMause, "Evolution of Childhood," pp. 31–38.

10. The fact that this led to traumatization, insanity, and even death did not halt the prevailing practices until the nineteenth century. DeMause reports the following story drawn from a woman's account of her friend's baby daughter whose nurse, not wanting the child to disturb her social plans for the evening, told the child that a "horrible black man" was hidden in the room waiting to catch her if she made a noise or left her bed. After constructing just such a huge, frightful figure and leaving it at the foot of the sleeping child's bed, the nurse went out. When she returned "she beheld the little girl sitting up in her bed, staring in an agony of terror at the fearful monster before her, both hands convulsively grasping her fair hair. *She was stone dead.*" Rhoda E. White, *From Infancy to Womanhood: A Book of Instruction for Young Mothers* (London, 1882), p. 31.

11. Ariès, however, has been criticized by several European scholars for developing an overgeneralized and mythicized portrayal of this period, failing to take account of several important exceptions found in the culture of the people. See Emmanuel LeRoy Ladurie's well-known study *Montaillou: Cathars and Catholics in a French Village, 1294–1324* (London: Scolar Press, 1978).

12. Ariès, *Centuries of Childhood*, pp. 38–39.

13. Ibid., p. 50.

14. Martin Hoyles discusses this issue in his Introduction to *Changing Childhood,* ed. Martin Hoyles (London: Writers and Readers Publishing Cooperative, 1979), p. 28.

15. Ibid., p. 25.

16. Ariès, *Centuries of Childhood*, p. 99. But A. J. Beekman cautions that Ariès's sweeping claims about the separation between childhood and adulthood in the bourgeois milieu are, in certain instances, not justified. See "Opkomst en Neergang van de Kinderwereld; Een Historische Illusie?" *Utrechtse Pedagogische Verhandelingen* 2, 3 (December 1979):43–55.

17. Translated from Gerald Mendel and Christiaan Vogt, *El Manifesto de la Educación* (Madrid: Siglio XXI, 1975), in Emilia Rojo, "Between Two Conflicting Cultures: A Phenomenological Participatory Investigation of the Enduring Survival of a Mexican American Community" (Ph.D. diss., University of Michigan, 1980), p. 144.

18. Shulamit Firestone, *The Dialectic of Sex: The Case for Feminist Revolution* (New York: Morrow, 1970).

19. Ibid., p. 97.

20. Ibid., p. 10.

21. Ibid., p. 263.

22. Kate Millet, *Sexual Politics* (Garden City, N.Y.: Doubleday, 1970).

23. Germaine Greer, *The Female Eunuch* (New York: McGraw-Hill, 1971).

24. Alice Rossi, "A Biosocial Perspective on Parenting," *Daedalus*, spring 1977, p. 13.

25. Ibid., p. 16.

26. Nancy Chodorow, *The Reproduction of Mothering: Psychoanalysis and the Sociology of Gender* (Berkeley: University of California Press, 1978).

27. Nancy Chodorow discusses this issue of Freud's misogyny and ideological bias in *The Reproduction of Mothering*, pp. 142–44.

28. Ibid., p. 142.

29. See ibid., pp. 13–30, for Chodorow's critique of the biology and role-training / socialization arguments.

30. This existential-phenomenological term originates with Heidegger, who used it to denote a "being there" as being consciously present in the world.

31. Peter Fuller, "Uncovering Childhood," in Hoyles, *Changing Childhood*, p. 88.

32. Ibid., p. 81.

33. Ibid. The term "historicity of childhood" is taken from Fuller's photo essay, "Uncovering Childhood."

34. Friedrich Engels, writing on childhood in the potteries in *The Condition of the Working Class in England* (Oxford: Basil Blackwell, 1971), p. 235.

35. However, a century later, despite entrenched laws against child labor, one only has to pay a visit to the migrant families in any of the large grower farms or agribusiness corporations in this country to find similar deplorable working conditions for adults and children alike. See Robert Coles, *Children of Crisis*, vol. 2: *Migrants, Share-croppers, Mountaineers* (Boston: Little, Brown, 1971), for excellent documentation of this widespread phenomenon.

36. This extremely apt metaphor is taken from Paulo Freire's work; for a discussion of "banking education" see *Pedagogy of the Oppressed* (New York: Seabury Press, 1970), chap. 2, and also *Pedagogy in Process: The Letters to Guinea-Bissau* (New York: Seabury Press, 1978).

37. For a fascinating account of the Cuban literacy campaign (as educational praxis), see Jonathan Kozol, *Children of the Revolution* (New York: Delacorte Press, 1978); and also for an account of his own involvement in Guinea-Bissau, see Freire, *Pedagogy in Process*.

38. Freire, *Pedagogy of the Oppressed*, p. 68.

39. Coles, "Children as Moral Observers."

40. Donald Vandenberg, *Being and Education* (Englewood Cliffs, N.J.: Prentice-Hall, 1971), p. 63.

41. W. H. Gillespie, "Aggression and Instinct Theory," *International Journal of Psychoanalysis* 52 (1971):155.

42. Anne Freud, "Comments on Aggression," *International Journal of Psychoanalysis* 53 (1972):163.

43. Roger D. Abrahams, *Positively Black* (Englewood Cliffs, N.J.: Prentice-Hall, 1970).

44. Rojo, "Between Two Conflicting Cultures."

45. Albert Bandura and Richard H. Walters, *Social Learning and Personality Development* (New York: Holt, Rinehart and Winston, 1963).

46. See Thomas Gordon's instant recipes in *T.E.T., Teacher Effectiveness Training* (New York: David McKay, 1977), and *P.E.T., Parent Effectiveness Training: The Tested New Way to Raise Responsible Children* (New York: New American Library, 1975).

47. Lawrence Kohlberg, "Moral Development," in *Collected Papers on Moral Development and Moral Education* (Cambridge, Mass.: Center for Moral Education, 1973).

48. Coles, *Children of Crisis*, vol. 1: *A Study of Courage and Fear* (New York: Delta, 1967).

49. Coles, *Children of Crisis*, vol. 2.

50. Coles, *Children of Crisis*, vol. 5: *Privileged Ones: The Well-off and the Rich in America* (New York: Little, Brown, 1977).

51. Coles, "Children as Moral Observers."

52. Martin Hoffman, "Empathy, Role Taking, Guilt, and Development of Altruistic Motives," in *Morality: Theory, Research, and Social Issues*, ed. Tom Likona (Holt, Rinehart and Winston, 1976), pp. 124–43; and "Causal Inference in Correlational Research: Discipline and Moral Development," in *Recent Studies in Cognitive and Social Development in Children*, ed. W. E. Fthenakis (Donauworth: Verlag Ludwig Auer, 1977), pp. 15–31.

53. Coles, "Children as Moral Observers."

54. Hans Georg Gadamer, *Philosophical Hermeneutics* (Berkeley: University of California Press, 1976), p. xix.

55. Max Van Manen discusses Buytendijk's formulation of the leitmotif of child phenomenology in an excellent article, "An Experiment in Educational Theorizing: The Utrecht School," *Interchange* 10, no. 1 (1978–79):58.

Chapter 2

1. Coles, *Children of Crisis*, vol. 2, pp. 25, 41.

2. Paulo Freire has used this term to describe an authentic educational process. I would think it applies as effectively to the research process. See *Pedagogy of the Oppressed*, chap. 3, for discussion of the "dialogical encounter."

3. Sigmund Koch, "Language Communities, Search Cells and the Psychological Studies," in *Nebraska Symposium on Motivation, 1975: Conceptual Foundations of Psychology*, ed. W. J. Arnold (Lincoln, Neb.: University of Nebraska, 1976), p. 486.

4. By quantitative, I refer to the current orientation toward measuring, quantifying, and computing facets of human experience; this ranges from the "soft" interview questionnaires to the "hard" technology of the computer.

5. Liam Hudson, *The Cult of the Fact* (London: Jonathan Cape, 1972).

6. The distinction between social science and human science is essentially one of intention, method, and assumptions about the nature of the human condition. This is elaborated later in the present chapter.

7. Maurice Merleau-Ponty, "Eye and Mind," in *The Primacy of Perception*, ed. James Edie (Evanston, Ill.: Northwestern University Press, 1964), p. 159.

8. Karl Mannheim, *Ideology and Utopia* (London: Routledge and Kegan Paul, 1946).

9. Samuel Sillen and Alexander Thomas, *Racism and Psychiatry* (New York: Brunner Mazel, 1972).

10. Jacques Ellul, "The Technological Order," in C. Mitcham and R. Mackey, eds., *Philosophy and Technology* (New York: Free Press, Macmillan, 1972).

11. Peter Berger et al., *The Homeless Mind* (New York: Vintage Books, 1973), chap. 1.

12. Paulo Freire, *Education for Critical Consciousness* (New York: Seabury, 1973).

13. Herbert Schiller, *Communication and Cultural Domination* (White Plains, N.Y.: M. E. Sharpe, 1976), p. 68.

14. Max Van Manen elaborates this point in his article, "An Experiment in Educational Theorizing: The Utrecht School," where he reviews the work of the Dutch phenomenologist A. J. Beekman. *Interchange* 10, no. 1 (1978–79):48–66.

15. Hans Georg Gadamer, "The Universality of the Hermeneutical Problem," *Philosophical Hermeneutics* (Berkeley: University of California Press, 1976), p. 11.

16. Ibid., p. xvi.

17. Ibid., pp. xix, xx.

18. See Van Manen, "An Experiment in Educational Theorizing."

19. Martin Heidegger's definition of "phenomenology" in "Sein und Zeit" discussed in J. Kockelmans, *Martin Heidegger: A First Introduction to His Philosophy* (Pittsburgh: Duquesne University Press, 1975).

20. Clifford Geertz, "Thick Description: Toward an Interpretive Theory of Culture," in *The Interpretation of Cultures* (New York: Basic Books, 1973), p. 23.

21. Jean-Paul Sartre, "Critique of Dialectical Reason," in R. D. Laing and D. Cooper, eds., *Reason and Violence* (New York: Vintage Books, 1971), p. 101.

22. Sartre, *The Emotions: Outline of a Theory* (New York: Philosophical Library, 1948).

23. Sartre, *Search for a Method* (New York: Vintage Books, 1968), p. 18.

24. Paulo Freire has described "conscientization" *(conscientização)* as the process of moving from a state of being submerged in reality, critically reflecting on that reality, and moving to a state of active intervention in that reality. Hence, critical thought + action = praxis. See *Pedagogy of the Oppressed*, chap. 3.

25. Athol Fugard, a South African playwright of remarkable vision and courage, writing on the "pure theatre experience" in the Introduction to *Statements* (Oxford: Oxford University Press, 1974).

26. William Blake, "Auguries of Innocence," in *Complete Writings of Blake*, ed. Geoffrey Keynes (London: Oxford University Press, 1969), p. 431.

27. Dylan Thomas, "Fern Hill," in *The Collected Poems of Dylan Thomas 1934–1952* (New York: New Directions, 1971), p. 178.

Chapter 3

1. Samuel Bowles, "Unequal Education and the Reproduction of the Social Division of Labor," in *Schooling in a Corporate Society*, ed. Carnoy Martin (New York: David McKay, 1972).

2. William Cave and Mark Chesler, "Education and Social Change: Romanticism Revisited," *Innovator* 7 (July 1976):19–20.

3. Jonathan Kozol, *The Night Is Dark and I am Far from Home* (New York: Bantam Books, 1975), pp. 10, 13.

4. The term "ideologization" first emerged during a conversation with Paulo Freire in Ann Arbor in 1979, and I am indebted to him for this insight into my study.

5. The term "daycare" is ambiguous, for it is used (1) as a generic term to refer to all forms of institutionalized childcare programs, and (2) to distinguish a daycare program from a nursery school—for example, where the program is more structured, more cognitively oriented, and only part-day. I use the term to refer to any *formal* childcare institution.

6. Most of the material for this section on the historical origins of daycare is derived from Margaret O'Brien Steinfels, *Who's Minding the Children?* (New York: Simon and Schuster, 1973).

7. Cited in ibid., p. 36.

8. Ibid., p. 45.

9. Ibid., p. 42.

10. Ibid., pp. 59, 60.

11. Ibid., p. 72.

12. Ibid., pp. 87, 88.

13. John Bowlby, *Maternal Care and Mental Health* (New York: Schocken Books, 1966).

14. René Spitz, "Hospitalism: An Inquiry into the Genesis of Psychiatric Conditions in Early Childhood," in Urie Bronfenbrenner et al., *Influences on Human Development* (Hinsdale, Ill.: Dryden Press, 1975).

15. Selma Fraiberg, *Every Child's Birthright: In Defense of Mothering* (New York: Basic Books, 1977), p. 62.

16. The findings of Kagan and his associates indicate that infants from intact and psychologically supportive families who experience good surrogate care from stable and nurturant caretakers in a challenging cognitive environment are not adversely affected by early daycare. However, as these researchers readily acknowledge, these results are based on the provision of high-quality care within a carefully contoured environment and should not be assumed to imply that *any* daycare context would produce the same consequences. See Jerome Kagan et al., *Infancy: Its Place In Human Development* (Cambridge: Harvard University Press, 1978), p. 265.

17. Children's House, a demonstration project of the Yale Child Study Center, and the Syracuse Children's Center are two notable examples.

18. Fraiberg, *Every Child's Birthright*, p. 87.

19. Beatrice M. Glickman and Nesha B. Springer, *Who Cares for the Baby?* (New York: Schocken Books, 1978), p. 11.

20. Mary Dublin Keyserling, *Windows on Daycare* (New York: National Council of Jewish Women, 1972).

21. Steinfels, *Who's Minding the Children?*

22. Keyserling, *Windows on Daycare*, p. 9.

23. Nancy B. Dearman and Valena White Plisko, *The Condition of Education* (Washington, D.C.: National Center for Educational Statistics, 1980).

24. Fraiberg, *Every Child's Birthright*, p. 141.

25. Clifford Geertz, "Thick Description: Toward an Interpretive Theory of Culture," in *The Interpretation of Cultures* (New York: Basic Books, 1973), p. 25.

26. In discussing early institutionalization, I refer only to a partial (daycare) as opposed to a total (orphanages, hospitals) institutionalization experience for young children.

27. Robert Coles, *Children of Crisis*, vol. 2, p. 37.

Chapter 4

1. Jules Henry, *Pathways to Madness* (New York: Vintage Books, 1973), pp. 11, 13.

2. Maurice Merleau-Ponty, *Phenomenology of Perception* (London: Routledge and Kegan Paul, 1962), p. 417.

3. Comments of a four-year-old from an "alternative, free" school who went to visit this school as a prospective student and decided he did not want to stay.

4. Jan Piaget, *The Construction of Reality in the Child* (New York: Basic Books, 1954).

Chapter 5

1. This was the only center during my two years of observation where I was specifically asked *not* to be a participant-observer and to remain seated outside the periphery of activity, interacting as little as possible with the children. For all intents and purposes, I was a "silent" observer at this preschool.

2. Maria Montessori, *The Secret of Childhood* (Calcutta: Orient Longmans, 1963), p. 208.

3. Montessori, *The Absorbent Mind* (Wheaton, Ill.: Theosophical Press, 1964).

4. Jean Piaget, *The Origins of Intelligence in Children* (New York: International University Press, 1952).

5. Montessori, *Secret of Childhood*.

6. Montessori, *Absorbent Mind*.

7. Piaget, *Origins of Intelligence*.

8. Jerome Bruner, "Play is Serious Business," *Psychology Today*, January 1975, pp. 80–83.

9. John Dewey and Evelyn Dewey, *Schools of Tomorrow* (New York: Dutton, 1915), p. 157.

10. "Given the functions of preventing internal change and struggling to survive, bureaucracies tend to devote much of their time to activities that prevent change." Jules Henry, *On Education* (New York: Vintage Books, 1972), p. 20.

Chapter 6

1. Rollo May, *Power and Innocence: A Search for the Sources of Violence* (New York: W. W. Norton, 1972), p. 243.

2. Jean-Paul Sartre, Preface to Frantz Fanon, *Wretched of the Earth* (New York: Grove Press, 1963), p. 24.

3. Herbert Gintis, "Alienation and Power," *Review of Radical Political Economics* 4 (Fall 1972):25.

4. Henry, *Pathways to Madness*, p. 101.

5. Joseph Featherstone, "Kentucky Fried Children," *New Republic* 163 (5, 12 September 1970):15.

6. Dearman and Plisko, *The Condition of Education* (1980), chap. 3.

7. Keyserling, *Windows on Daycare*, p. 50.

8. Fraiberg, *Every Child's Birthright*, p. 80.

Chapter 7

1. See, for example, the account of the Ik tribe in Colin Turnbull, *The Mountain People* (New York: Simon and Schuster, 1972).

2. Merleau-Ponty, *Phenomenology of Perception*, p. 417.

3. Eliot Liebow, *Tally's Corner* (Boston: Little, Brown, 1967).

4. Jack had been previously diagnosed by the Psychology Clinic as "semiretarded" with the mental age of a toddler! He made remarkable progress during those one-and-a-half years.

5. Ralf Dahrendorf, "Out of Utopia: Toward a Reorientation of Sociological Analysis," *American Journal of Sociology* 64 (1958):115–27.

6. Abrahams, *Positively Black*.

7. I found it interesting that the white grandmother appeared to have adopted many of the norms, speech patterns, and interaction styles of her two black consociates.

8. The discussion about the meaning of the grandmothers' presence and the related themes that have emerged in this chapter are due, in no small part, to the many dialogues with friend and colleague Bill Cave, whose insights were invaluable to me.

Chapter 8

1. A. S. Neill, *Summerhill: A Radical Approach to Child Rearing* (New York: Hart, 1960), p. 12.

2. The role and responsibility of the teacher is a thorny issue, constantly wrestled with by those who wish to create a climate for liberating education. The complexities of this question and the importance of recognizing one's responsibilities in this regard were brought home forcefully to me in 1978, during a seminar with Paulo Freire, when he stated, with great conviction, "I have nothing *to deny* that I am a teacher!"

3. Frithjof Bergmann, *On Being Free* (Notre Dame, Ind.: University of Notre Dame Press, 1977), p. 110.

Chapter 9

1. Vandenberg, *Being and Education,* p. 63.

2. Ibid., p. 60.

3. Maurice Merleau-Ponty, *The Structure of Behavior* (Boston: Beacon Press, 1963).

4. Sartre, in *Being and Nothingness,* part 4 (London: University Paperbacks, 1969), has categorized the "en-soi" (in-itself), as the passive, other-defined, inert essence of the human being, while the "pour-soi" (for-itself), represents the active consciousness, the authentic mode of existence. Sartre claimed that our being embodies both the pour-soi and the en-soi housed in a perpetual dialectic of consciousness, but that we live in continued danger of the pour-soi collapsing into the en-soi, i.e., the antithesis not negating the given socially prescribed thesis. It is the pour-soi that possesses the power of reflexive consciousness, which permits us to critically reflect upon our social reality.

5. M. J. Langeveld, the Dutch phenomenologist, has been the major contributor to the phenomenology of childhood and play. See *Studien zur Anthropologie des Kindes* (Tübingen: Max Niemeyer Verlag, 1956).

6. For useful references on the corporate schooling phenomenon, see the series of readings, *Schooling in a Corporate Society,* ed. Martin Carnoy (New York: David McKay, 1972).

7. Ivan Illich, *Deschooling Society* (New York: Harper and Row, 1971).

8. Charles Silberman, *Crisis in the Classroom: The Remaking of American Education* (New York: Random House, 1970).

9. Merleau-Ponty, *Phenomenology of Perception,* p. 427.

10. Vandenberg, *Being and Education,* p. 66.

11. F. J. Buytendijk, "Experienced Freedom and Moral Freedom in the Child's Consciousness," *Educational Theory* 3 (January 1953):1–13.

12. Vandenberg, *Being and Education*, p. 73.

13. Sartre; see note 4 above.

14. Howard Saul Becker, *Outsiders* (London: Collier Macmillan, 1966), p. 9.

15. Erving Goffman, *Asylums* (Chicago: Aldine, 1962). Thomas Scheff has written a fascinating book on the *ascription of deviance* showing, in fact, through his analysis of psychiatric and legal committal procedures, that the patient adopts such a role determined by "audience" reaction. See *Being Mentally Ill: A Sociological Theory* (London: Weidenfeld and Nicholson, 1966).

16. William Ryan, *Blaming the Victim* (New York: Pantheon Books, 1971).

17. Freire, *Pedagogy of the Oppressed*, pp. 62–63.

18. Jean Piaget, *To Understand Is To Invent: The Future of Education* (New York: Viking Press, 1974), p. 7.

19. Henry, *On Education*, p. 20.

20. Mark Chesler and James Crowfoot, "Toward a Conflict Model for Understanding the Organization of Schooling in America," Report to Northwest Regional Laboratories, Portland, Ore. (Ann Arbor: Community Resources Ltd., 1975), p. 9.

21. I am indebted to Frances Hawkins for her insightful comments about this issue during a personal conversation at the University of Michigan, fall 1980.

22. Klaus Riegel, "The Dialectics of Human Development," *American Psychologist* 31 (October 1976):689–700.

23. Vandenberg, *Being and Education*, p. 71.

24. Thanks are due here to my colleague Biff Barritt for the above insight during one such conflictful argument.

25. Joel Spring, *Education and the Rise of the Corporate State* (Boston: Beacon Press, 1972), pp. 164–65.

26. Samuel Bowles and Herbert Gintis, "IQ in the U.S. Class Structure," *Social Policy*, November/December 1972, January/February 1973, pp. 63–96.

27. Herbert Gintis, "Alienation and Power," *Review of Radical Political Economics* 4, no. 5 (Fall 1972).

28. Alice Lake, "The Day Care Business," in *The Day Care Book*, ed. V. Breitbart (New York: Alfred A. Knopf, 1974), p. 37.

29. Ibid., p. 38.

30. Keyserling, *Windows on Daycare*, p. 64.

31. Ibid., p. 14.

Chapter 10

1. Urie Bronfenbrenner, *Two Worlds of Childhood: U.S. and U.S.S.R.* (New York: Russell Sage Foundation, 1970), p. 165.

2. Sartre, *Search for a Method*, p. 29.

3. I have borrowed this term from Russell Jacoby's book by the same title. See *Social Amnesia* (Boston: Beacon Press, 1975).

4. Bronfenbrenner, *Two Worlds of Childhood*, p. 177.

5. Jacques Ellul, "The Technological Order," in C. Mitcham and R. Mackey, eds., *Philosophy and Technology* (New York: Free Press Macmillan, 1972).

6. Firestone, *The Dialectic of Sex: The Case for Feminist Revolution*.

7. Peter Berger and Thomas Luckmann, *The Social Construction of Reality* (New York: Anchor Books, 1967), p. 134.

8. Ibid., p. 138.

9. Ibid., p. 132.

10. Robert Coles and Jane Hallowell Coles, *Women of Crisis: Lives of Struggle and Hope* (New York: Delta/Seymour L. Lawrence, 1978), pp. 235–37.

11. Fraiberg, *Every Child's Birthright*, p. 104.

12. Freire, *Pedagogy of the Oppressed*, p. 92.

13. Ibid., p. 93.

14. Much of the information for this section is taken from Marvin Leiner, *Children Are the Revolution: Day Care in Cuba* (New York: Viking Press, 1974).

15. Ibid., p. 18.

16. Ibid., p. 21.

17. The two types of preschool centers in Cuba are described by Leiner as (a) *jardines*—freer, less structured, more "play oriented," eighteen months to five years; (b) *circulos*—more structured, directed learning, planned schedules, emphasis on cleanliness, forty-five days to five years.

18. Ruth Sidel, *Women and Child Care in China* (Baltimore, Md.: Penguin Books, 1973), p. 102.

19. William Kessen, ed., *Childhood in China* (New Haven: Yale University Press, 1975), p. 55.

20. Ibid., p. 63.

21. Bronfenbrenner, *Two Worlds of Childhood*.

22. Cited in Stephanie Urdang, "Precondition for Victory: Women's Liberation in Mozambique and Guinea-Bissau," *Issue* 8, no. 1 (Spring 1978):25.

23. See Amilcar Cabral, "The Role of Culture in the Liberation Struggle," speech delivered to the UNESCO Conference in Paris, 3–7 July 1972.

24. Hilda Scott, *Women and Socialism* (London: Alison and Busby, 1976), chap. 8.

25. Bruno Bettelheim, *Children of the Dream* (New York: Macmillan, 1969).

26. I am indebted to Moncrief Cochran from the Department of Human Development and Family Studies at Cornell University for the following information about Sweden obtained during a personal conversation in May 1981.

27. Bronfenbrenner discussed these issues in a lecture entitled "The Ecology of Education" at the University of Michigan, Ann Arbor, 5 March 1981.

28. The term "child-friendly" was used by Ton Beekman, the Dutch phenomenologist, during one of his visits to the University of Michigan in 1978.

29. Two such centers with which I am familiar are Corntree Childcare Cooperative, Ann Arbor, Michigan (where I, together with my family, was involved for six years), and the Bank Street College of Education Parent-Child Cooperative, New York.

30. Cited in a letter of Karl Marx to his daughter Jenny, in David McLellan, *Karl Marx: His Life and Thought* (New York: Harper and Row, 1973), p. 449. This excellent biography discusses the aging Marx and his love for his grandchildren.

Index